THE
REST
REVOLUTION

The Power of Rest for Women

HEATHER BOERSMA

THE SELF PUBLISHING AGENCY

Heather Boersma
The Rest Revolution

Copyright © 2025 by Heather Boersma
First Edition

Softcover ISBN 978-1-0693895-0-3
eBook ISBN 978-1-0693895-1-0

All rights reserved under International and Pan-American Copyright Conventions.
Manufactured in Canada.

No part of this publication may be reproduced, stored in, or introduced into a retrieval system, transmitted in any form or by any means (electronic, mechanical, photocopying, recording, or otherwise), and/or otherwise used in any manner for purposes of training artificial intelligence technologies to generate text, including, without limitation, technologies that are capable of generating works in the same style or genre as this publication, without the prior written permission of the publisher.

This book is sold subject to the condition that it shall not, by way of trade or otherwise, be lent, resold, hired out, or otherwise circulated without the publisher's prior written consent in any form of binding, cover, or condition other than that in which it was published.

Book Cover Design | Tracy Hetherington
Book Interior Design | Petya Tsankova
Editor | Judith Doyle
Publishing Management | TSPA The Self Publishing Agency, Inc.

To the woman who is so exhausted she's not sure she can go on.
Thank you for showing up.
Your courage and commitment inspire me every day.

This one's for you.

TABLE OF CONTENTS

INTRODUCTION: The Case for Rest	1
PART 1: THE REST CRISIS	9
CHAPTER 1: The Cost of the Hustle	13
CHAPTER 2: Rest is Not a Nap	19
CHAPTER 3: Rest is Not a Reward	25
PART 2: THE SHIFT TO REST	29
CHAPTER 4: Best Friend Yourself	33
CHAPTER 5: Rest for Your Body	45
CHAPTER 6: Rest for Your Mind	55
CHAPTER 7: Feel Your Feelings	65
CHAPTER 8: Living From Not For	73
CHAPTER 9: Rest Is Productive	81
PART 3: LIVING THE REVOLUTION	87
CHAPTER 10: Values, Goals, and Scheduling	93
CHAPTER 11: Burnout-Proof Your Life	109
CHAPTER 12: Rest Is the Revolution	123
RESOURCES	129
ACKNOWLEDGEMENTS	133
ABOUT THE AUTHOR	135

INTRODUCTION

The Call to Rest

By the time I boarded my second flight of the day, I knew something wasn't right. Travel days always felt long, but this one started especially early and it was already getting late. I was heading home to my three- and one-year-old who I missed and felt guilty for leaving. I knew they were well taken care of at home with my husband, but I felt the pull to get home as soon as possible.

I walked over to a cafe and ordered a peppermint tea, hoping it would calm my churning stomach. I felt a nervous energy I couldn't quite put a finger on. It wasn't the flight—I've never been afraid of getting into a small metal tube that will hurl me through the sky at high speeds. And it wasn't that I was sick, or at least I didn't think so. But I felt nauseous and waves of heat were rolling over my entire body.

Maybe I didn't want hot tea after all.

As I took my seat on the plane, the sensations in my body intensified. I felt like I couldn't focus my eyes and my heart was racing. I buckled my seat belt and used my free hand to check for the pulse under my chin. Bum, bum, bum. The rush of blood raced through the vein just below my fingers, faster and faster. I set my tea on the ground between my feet and squeezed my eyes shut.

"Just breathe," I whispered to myself. "In and out."

Despite my self-coaching, I felt my vision going blurry and my fingers starting to tingle. Was I going to pass out right here on this airplane full of strangers? Forget passing out, was I about to die?

I reached up for the steward call button and pressed it firmly. He came over immediately and I motioned for him to come close so my seatmate wouldn't hear my question.

"Do you have oxygen on this flight?"

"Excuse me, ma'am?"

"Oxygen? Do you have an oxygen mask? I think I'm about to pass out."

He leaned in a little closer, his hand gently resting on my arm. "We do, but if we give it to you, you'll be met by paramedics upon landing. Would you still like me to get it for you?"

As much as the racing heart and tingling fingers were freaking me out, the idea of being wheeled off the plane on a stretcher was even worse.

"No, no, that's okay. I'm fine actually," I said, wringing my hands together in my lap.

"But if you have some anti-nausea medication, I'll take that."

Before this flight, I was still telling myself I was okay. But I wasn't. I was living in constant overdrive, and my body was finally demanding the rest I'd been refusing to give it. But what had led me to this breaking point?

To really understand why I was having a panic attack on the airplane, we need to rewind the story nearly 20 years earlier, right after I got engaged to my husband, Alex. I was still living in my childhood home and excitedly planning my upcoming wedding.

On an average afternoon in the fall of 2007, my parents called a family meeting. In attendance at this very official feeling meeting was my mom and dad, my brother and sister-in-law, and my fiancé and I. My parents weren't really the type to call family meetings, so I was feeling the buzz of anxiety in my body.

"Your mom has breast cancer," my dad said, not mincing any words.

At the time I knew very little about breast cancer and my mind immediately jumped to the worst-case scenario—my mom was going to die. I don't remember the rest of that meeting, but I do remember crying myself to sleep that night, imaging my life without her.

But breast cancer didn't claim my mom's life. After surgery and chemotherapy, she survived, and is now cancer free. However, another result of that experience, was the discovery that my family carried the BRCA2 "breast cancer" gene. Because of this my mom chose to have preventative surgeries: a double mastectomy reconstruction and a hysterectomy. Watching her go through that process was one of the hardest things I've ever experienced.

One memory that is etched into my mind was a day or two after her reconstruction surgery. Alex and I were recently married and enjoying the honeymoon phase of our relationship. I went to my parents' home to check in on my mom while my dad was at work. I remember going into my childhood bedroom, now turned guest room, where my mom was sleeping on a recliner chair. Part of her recovery was that she couldn't lay down flat for the first few weeks.

I don't remember a lot, but I do remember the drains coming out of her body and the cap covering her head, still mostly bald from chemotherapy. She looked weak and sick, even though she was very much on the road to recovery. And she was nauseous—so very nauseous. Suddenly her eyes opened and she weakly asked me to come over and help her sit up. She needed to vomit and couldn't sit up on her own. It was a moment I will never forget watching my own mom, who always seemed so strong and sure, show her humanity. The helped had become the helper.

Since my mom was a BRCA2 carrier, I was given the option to be tested as well. I had a 50/50 chance of being a carrier myself. I'd always joked that I was more like my dad than my mom, and as I waited for my results, I prayed that would be the case.

Introduction

Before my airplane panic attack, I received the results from my genetic testing. I still remember walking into the office of the genetic counsellor's office, Alex by my side. She handed me a piece of paper, the words on the page blurred together. I was a carrier. Even though I'd been mentally preparing for this possibility, it felt like a punch to the gut. I'd spent the past six years witnessing my mom's exhausting cancer journey, and quite frankly, I was filled with fear that her story would be mine as well.

Being BRCA2 positive meant I had an increased risk of breast and ovarian cancer—not the kind of news a 30-year-old mom of two expects to hear. It was at this time I started telling myself the story, *"I'm going to get cancer."*

Shortly after receiving these results, I witnessed my uncle, whose children were like my own siblings, quickly deteriorate and pass away from cancer. My internal story escalated to *"I'm going to get cancer and die."*

On top of the stress of my health diagnosis, and the grief of the first real loss I'd experienced, another force was at play, draining me of energy and joy for life.

That force was my people-pleasing tendencies. I was constantly hyperaware of how other people were feeling. I spent most of my free time and energy (which wasn't much) trying to keep everyone happy. I hated the thought of anyone I loved or ever knew being upset or unhappy, especially with me.

I'd learned early on that my greatest asset was my ability to get things done. When I said yes, I was praised. When I volunteered for an opportunity, I was affirmed. People-pleasing became my full-time job, and I was killing it! But it was killing me.

In my quest to please the people around me, I'd lost sight of myself. As a mom of two young children, I spent my days guiding little limbs through soft cotton clothing and wiping sticky substances off chubby fingers and cheeks. I rarely got enough sleep to feel clear-headed, and even my mom, who rarely spends money on anything but the necessities, was suggesting I pay for weekly house cleaning. I'd packed my life so full of productivity that I was on the edge of burnout, and I couldn't even see it. All I cared about was filling my calendar with more "important things"—another speaking event or an opportunity to build my platform—and it was starting to take a toll. Add on the genetic testing results and the loss of my uncle and suddenly what had been working wasn't working anymore.

I'd recently taken on a new project, writing and hosting a television show for teen girls. But between raising two kids, maintaining a marriage, keeping a home, speaking, writing, and now walking through the grief of loss—my edges were starting to fray. Not just my edges actually. It was like a thread had been pulled from the middle of me and I was unravelling in every direction. And the more I said yes, the more I fell apart.

I'm writing this book because I suspect my story is not uncommon. The more people I meet, the more I see the frayed edges and the gaping holes in all of us. And even though we can't prevent the hard things life throws at us, we can choose the approach we take to dealing with them. And not just dealing with the challenges, but the way we face our everyday life.

The approach I want to offer you, my dear reader, is the approach I've spent the last ten years cultivating—since that first panic attack on the airplane. It's the approach of rest.

Within the pages of this book, you will find the tools you need to live a more rested life. The tools are not complicated or even time consuming. They are simple, backed with science, and easy to apply to your everyday life. As I share my story of healing from burnout and the stories of my clients who have embraced rest and reaped the rewards, I hope you feel encouraged to not give up.

But this book isn't just about adding more naps or self-care days to your calendar. It's about something deeper. It's about reclaiming your life from the lies of hustle culture—the ones that tell you your worth is tied to your productivity. Learning to rest is an act of rebellion against a world that demands you earn your belonging through exhaustion. It's a quiet revolution, and it begins inside you.

This isn't a self-help book. It's a love letter to the tired part of you—the part that's been carrying too much for too long and is ready to finally set it down. And it's a war cry to the wild part of you—the part that was never meant to be tamed by hustle and striving. The part that's still alive beneath the exhaustion, waiting to be set free.

If you're tired of the hustle, overwhelmed by the endless to-dos, and aching for a different way to live, pull up a chair, my friend. There is good news for you.

The revolution of rest is already waiting inside you.

But before we can live the revolution, we need to understand why we resist rest so fiercely. Why does something so simple feel so impossible? That's where our journey begins.

PART 1
THE REST CRISIS

Burnout isn't just feeling tired—it's feeling empty. It's waking up already overwhelmed and carrying the weight of that exhaustion into every part of your life. It's snapping at your kids because you're running on fumes. It's cancelling plans with friends because you simply don't have the energy. It's lying awake at night, worrying about everything you didn't get done, and feeling like no matter how hard you try, it's never enough. And so many of us are experiencing this: according to Gallup in 2023, 33% of working women reported feeling burned out very often or always.

And if you've been living that way for long enough, it starts to feel normal—even though deep down, you know something precious is slipping away. Burnout doesn't just drain your energy. It steals your focus, your creativity, and your joy. It robs you of the moments you can't get back—moments with the people you love, and the dreams you once couldn't wait to build.

The Maslach Burnout Inventory (MBI), one of the most widely used tools for assessing burnout, highlights how it impacts three areas: emotional exhaustion, depersonalization, and a reduced sense of accomplishment. The thing is these symptoms can creep in so slowly that they start to feel normal. Feeling drained, disconnected from others, and doubting yourself becomes the default setting.

We've all been there, completely exhausted, but still pushing through. We tell ourselves we don't have a choice, that we must keep going. But the truth is, we do have a choice. We can step out of the cycle of hustle and exhaustion. We can choose a life rooted in rest. But first, we need to take an honest look at what our resistance to rest is really costing us.

CHAPTER 1

The Cost of the Hustle

For me, hustle was a way of life that started much younger that you might think. It wasn't something I ever consciously chose, but rather the way I adapted to survive in the precarious social situations I found myself in early in life. As a young child I was incredibly imaginative and free spirited. I chatted incessantly to whoever would listen and if no one was around, I'd talk to myself or my imaginary friends. I was energetic and loud, and my parents, who were considering a third child, decided to stick with two after a couple years of raising me. They loved me fiercely, but I think I tired them out just a little.

In elementary school, my big personality and constant chatter became an obstacle to me building friendships. Rather than drawing people in, I seemed to repel them. Little Heather, who just wanted to be loved and known, found herself on the outside of the in-crowd.

There were moments when I felt included with my peers, but the moments that stand out most are the ones when I spent recess leaning against an overturned metal garbage can at the edge of the playground, watching the other kids having fun. Rather than being embraced for who I was, I felt like I was too much and not enough at the same time.

It was during these years that my future burnout really started. Rather than believing I was worthy the way I was, I felt I had to hustle for love and belonging. I learned that if I edited my true personality, I could get a better reaction from my peers. I became a shape shifter, changing myself to fit the people and places I found myself in.

This pattern carried on from elementary into junior high. Even though changing myself seemed to help me fit in, what I didn't realize was how exhausting it was. Trying to be someone other than your authentic self comes at a cost, doesn't it?

This is really the core of hustle culture. It's not so much about being busy, it's about being someone other than who you truly are. Living in a way that doesn't match what matters most to you. And that hustle, it will catch up to you, just like it did to me on the airplane, many years later.

When did the hustle start for you? When did you start believing that being yourself wasn't safe? When did you start editing yourself to fit in and earn the love and belonging you were wired for? When did you start the exhausting battle for your worthiness?

The thing with hustle is that it's not sustainable. It leads to burnout every single time, and it does this in three ways:

1. It creates emotional exhaustion because you start ignoring your emotions instead of feeling them.
2. It creates depersonalization by confirming that your authentic self isn't lovable, and you need to change who you are to belong.

3. It robs you of the joy of your personal accomplishments by telling you that what you've done is never enough.

My hustle continued growing year after year and really got a boost the summer after I turned seventeen. Ironically this upswing in shape-shifting happened in a place where I'd always felt free to be myself—summer camp. I started attending summer camp when I was in Grade 1 and hadn't missed a year since. Summer camp was my happy place. It was a place where my big personality had space to run. If I felt like an outcast at school, I felt like a superstar at camp.

But this summer was different because this summer I met a boy, and for the first time ever, the boy I liked actually liked me back. He seemed drawn to my sassy personality and love for adventure. He laughed at my jokes and didn't seem to mind my constant chatter. And before the summer ended, I had fallen in love. Young love, yes, but love nonetheless.

It seemed like the beginning of a fairy tale romance I'd been dreaming of, and there were definitely some beautiful moments. But underneath all the sweetness, something familiar was happening again. I was losing pieces of myself. I was shrinking, adjusting, and changing myself to be chosen and stay chosen. Even in love, the hustle was still alive and well.

Early on, I remember him telling me, "I'm just not that fired up about you." It hit me harder than I let on. Somewhere deep inside, I translated those words into a story I would carry for years: *You're not enough.* Still, I stayed. On and off, for four years, we kept trying—and failing—to make it work. Each time we broke up, I tried to edit myself into someone more lovable. Each time we got back together, I hoped maybe this time, I would be enough.

I still remember the day it finally ended for good. We were sitting on a hill overlooking the water at camp, the place that had always felt like home to me. He stared straight ahead, sunglasses covering whatever emotion might have been hiding in his eyes. I looked at him and said, "Either we're working toward something, or we're done. I can't do this back and forth anymore." Without hesitation or emotion he said, "I guess we're done then." And just like that, it was over.

I sat there for a long time, the wind moving off the water, trying to hold it together. It felt like the ground beneath me had shifted. But somewhere deep inside I knew this wasn't just about losing him. It was about something bigger. It was the beginning of letting go of the belief that I had to hustle for love. It was a crack forming in the foundation of striving I had built my life on.

Saying "enough" that day was one of the first steps I ever took toward rest. Not the kind of rest you find from taking a nap or going on vacation, but the deeper kind: being at rest with myself. At rest with my worth. At rest with the truth that I didn't have to shape-shift to be loved.

At the time, I didn't see it for what it was. But looking back now, I can see clearly: that ending was actually a beginning—the first quiet movement toward a different kind of life.

As you think about your own story, I wonder: what has the hustle been costing you? What parts of yourself have you been handing over, hoping to earn love, success, or approval? Have you quieted your voice in meetings? Buried your ideas to make others comfortable? Said yes when your whole body was begging you to say no? Shrunk yourself to fit into spaces you were never meant to fit into?

What would it look like to start finding rest—not just in your schedule, but in your soul? What would it feel like to stop striving for worthiness and start living from it? To believe you are already enough—not because of what you produce or perform, but simply because you exist? To live at rest with yourself, just as you are?

But learning to live at rest isn't just about giving yourself permission—it's about facing the fears and resistance that rise up when you try. As I discovered, even when I wanted to rest, my body and mind didn't make it easy.

CHAPTER 2

Rest Is Not a Nap

Resting should be easy, right? It's something we were born to do. The average person spends 26 years of their life sleeping, for goodness' sake! For how much we talk about needing a nap or wishing for a vacation, it's a wonder that when we finally take time to rest, we struggle so much to enjoy it.

After the airplane panic attack, everything in me knew I couldn't keep living the way I had been. What I didn't know at the time was that it would mark the beginning of a much deeper journey—one that wasn't just about slowing down my calendar but about coming back home to myself. At first, I thought the solution was simple: cancel a few things, take better care of myself, book a pedicure, have an afternoon off. But I quickly learned that true rest isn't something you squeeze into your schedule once a month. It's not an activity you add to your to-do list. Rest is a whole new way of living.

I started seeing a counsellor and checked in with my family doctor, who prescribed medication I could take if another panic attack happened. But instead of getting better, things seemed to get worse. When I tried to slow down and simplify my life, I became even more anxious. I remember booking a pedicure at a local spa—something that sounded like absolute luxury for a mom of two toddlers. But as I slipped into the plush robe in the spa change room, I felt the familiar rush of panic rising. Here I was, about to enjoy an afternoon of rest and relaxation, and instead, I was popping a Lorazepam tablet under my tongue just to be able to get through it.

And it wasn't just that one moment. There was also the trip to Mexico—a much-anticipated family vacation I thought would finally be the "reset" I needed. I imagined sunshine, ocean breezes, lazy afternoons by the pool. I thought if I could just get away from my real life, I would finally find peace. But even on the beach, surrounded by beauty, my mind raced. What if one of the kids got sick? What if something went wrong? I lay in a lounge chair, staring at the endless turquoise waves, and felt my chest tighten instead of soften. No amount of palm trees or frozen margaritas could fix the storm inside me. That's when it hit me: rest isn't about vacating your life. Rest is about coming home to yourself. And if you aren't at home inside your own heart, no vacation will be long enough or far enough to heal you.

When was the last time you truly rested—and how did it feel? I'm not talking about taking a nap, though I do love sleep. Especially those twenty-minute naps where you wake up drooling on the pillow. You know it's a good one when there's drool. I'm talking about resting while you're awake. Sitting down with no phone in your hand, no to-do list running through your mind, no plan to jump up and tackle. Can you remember a moment like that in the last week or month? And if you can, how long did it last before you reached for your phone or found something to "fix" around the house? Was it five minutes? Ten? Maybe just two?

How does it feel when you finally slow down? Are you able to relax and enjoy it or does it trigger guilt, anxiety, or even panic? Why is resting so dang hard for us?

In 2023, a meta-analysis of over 91 studies found that fatigue is one of the top five health complaints reported globally in primary healthcare. We're tired. All of us. Not just physically, but emotionally and spiritually too. This isn't just a you problem. And this is exactly why we need a Rest Revolution.

Merriam-Webster defines rest as "freedom from activity or labor; a state of motionlessness or inactivity." The first part of that definition sounds pretty good to me: "freedom from labor"—yes, please. But the second part, if I'm honest, doesn't sound so appealing: "a state of motionlessness or inactivity." It doesn't sound like rest. It sounds like a perfect opportunity for anxiety to sneak in.

If rest is what we're craving, why are we so resistant to actually doing it? Because most of us have misunderstood rest. Rest isn't about what you're doing or not doing. Rest is about how you're being. And the enemy of rest isn't busyness. The enemy of rest is unworthiness.

We're not hustling for the sake of being busy. We're hustling to prove something. To earn something. To finally feel like we're enough. What has us running around like chickens with our heads cut off isn't a love for chaos. It's fear—fear that if we stop producing, stop performing, stop proving ourselves, the love will dry up. The admiration will disappear. The belonging will vanish.

I learned this young. When I was twelve years old, I realized that the more I did, the more validation I received. I wasn't missing love at home—but at school, it was another story. From grades two to six, I was bullied. Sometimes it was being excluded, sometimes it was being laughed at in front of my classmates. It stung deeply. As young children, we crave belonging the way our bodies crave oxygen. And when we don't find it, we start making bargains. I'll be quieter. I'll be better. I'll be more helpful. I'll do more.

I turned to my church community to find acceptance. At first, just being part of youth group felt good. But it wasn't just attending that changed things—it was volunteering. You need someone to sing with the toddlers in the nursery? I'm in. A teen girl for the Christmas play? Pick me! A team leader for the fundraiser? Absolutely. The more I said yes, the more affirmation I received. Even though part of me knew I was loved for who I was, another part started to believe that love had to be earned.

Without realizing it, I tied my worthiness to my productivity. And that addiction—to being needed, to being useful—ran the show for the next two decades.

I'm curious: where did the productivity addiction start for you? Maybe it was the way your parents praised you when you behaved perfectly. Maybe it was the teachers who lit up when you aced an assignment—or the heavy silence when you didn't. Maybe it was the love that felt just a little out of reach unless you were performing, helping, succeeding.

However it began, here's the truth: you weren't made for nonstop hustling. You were made for wholeness. And neuroscience backs that up. When we rest, our brain engages in a beautiful process called neuroplasticity—reorganizing itself, forming new neural pathways that help us learn, solve problems, adapt, and heal. Far from being wasted time, rest is when some of our most critical growth happens.

We'll dive deeper into the science later, but for now, hear this: rest isn't weakness. It isn't indulgence. It's not something lazy people do when they have nothing better going on. And it's definitely not just a nap. Rest is essential. It's the foundation we rebuild our lives on—the place where healing, growth, and real strength begin.

True rest isn't just a break from your life. It's the way you learn to live your life—fully awake, fully alive, and fully yourself.

CHAPTER 3

Rest Is Not a Reward

Have you ever caught yourself thinking, "I'll rest after I finish this last thing"? Or told yourself you didn't deserve to slow down because there was still so much left to do? You're not alone. Most of us have been taught that rest is something we must earn—not something we inherently deserve.

We tie our worth to our productivity, believing the busier we are, the more valuable we must be. And underneath that belief, there's often a deeper, quieter feeling: guilt. Guilt that rises the moment we stop moving. Guilt that whispers, "You haven't done enough yet." Guilt that keeps us stuck in the hustle even when our bodies and souls are begging to slow down.

But here's the truth: rest is not a reward. It's not something you have to earn through exhaustion or accomplishment. It's your birthright. And reclaiming that truth changes everything.

Instead of asking, "Have I done enough work to deserve a rest?", we can ask, "Have I had enough rest to create my best work?"

That's a powerful shift, isn't it? But making that shift isn't easy. Because most of us have been carrying guilt about resting for as long as we can remember.

I remember it hitting me especially hard when I became a mom. How could I possibly justify taking a nap when the house was a mess, and the laundry was piling up? There was always something else to do. And not just the practical things—the invisible expectations too. The moms on Instagram making homemade organic baby food. The moms posting their six-week postpartum body transformations. Meanwhile, I was trying to keep tiny humans alive on two hours of sleep, wondering if I was already failing them.

It took me until my third baby to finally realize the mess could wait, but the nap couldn't. Because we can't give what we haven't first received.

If we want to love our people well, build businesses, raise families, or dream new dreams, we can't keep running on fumes. Rest doesn't steal from our ambition—it fuels it. It doesn't slow us down—it strengthens us for the journey ahead.

But breaking free from guilt isn't just about trying harder. It's about understanding where that guilt comes from.

We live in a culture that glorifies productivity. Especially among women, the expectation is clear: be everything to everyone. Achieve. Excel. Serve. Smile. Stay small. Keep going.

For many of us, especially millennial women who grew up in high-pressure environments, the link between productivity and worthiness runs deep. From a young age, success was celebrated. Slowness was suspect. Rest was something you had to earn with exceptional performance.

So it's no wonder that even today, an empty afternoon can feel uncomfortable. An unfinished to-do list can feel like a moral failure. Rest can feel like rebellion.

And in some ways, it is.

Rest is a rebellion against the culture of hustle that says your value is measured by how much you can do without breaking. Rest is a revolution against the story that says you must earn your belonging through exhaustion.

But even rebellion takes practice. Because for most of us, rest doesn't feel safe right away. Productivity feels safer. Hustling feels more familiar. Rest can feel like standing in a river without swimming—terrifying, vulnerable, exposed.

That's why we have to build trust inside our own bodies. We have to practice rest in small, courageous ways. Take a thirty-minute nap instead of folding another load of laundry. Leave work on time instead of staying late to prove your dedication. Tell a client, "I'll respond Monday morning," and close your laptop for the weekend.

Each time you do, you build evidence. Evidence that rest is safe. Evidence that your life doesn't fall apart when you step back. Evidence that you are still loved, still worthy, still enough.

Over time, the guilt softens. Over time, rest begins to feel not like a guilty pleasure but like a deep remembering. Like coming home.

When my clients first begin practising rest, they often panic a little. They tell me, "I have so much free time now—I don't even know what to do with it." And I smile, because I know what's happening. They're not just changing their schedules, they're changing their lives. They're stepping outside of hustle culture and learning how to live differently—more fully, more freely, more human.

James Suzman reminds us that for most of human history, people worked about fifteen hours a week and spent the rest of their time living—playing, creating, connecting. Our nervous systems were designed for that rhythm, not the relentless pace we call normal today.

No wonder we feel guilty slowing down. No wonder we feel lost when we finally do. But on the other side of that discomfort is something worth fighting for: a life built on rest, not rush.

Rest isn't the reward for finishing your life. Rest is what fuels you to live it.

PART 2
THE SHIFT TO REST

Hustle isn't just about being busy—it's about being disconnected from yourself. And burnout isn't just about feeling tired—it's about feeling lost. That's why stepping into a truly rested life requires more than a new planner or a better morning routine. It requires a new way of seeing yourself.

This next part of the journey is about the inner work—the mindset shifts, the belief healing, the quiet transformations happening under the surface. Because you can't live differently until you believe differently. And you, my friend, are ready.

Research backs this up. A 2023 study by Vlasceanu, Van Bavel, and Coman found that our beliefs act like blueprints for our lives, shaping the choices we make, how motivated we feel, and how we respond when challenges come. When those beliefs shift—whether through learning, reflection, or new experiences—our actions naturally start to follow.

For example, if you start to believe you're capable of balancing work and family life, you're more likely to make decisions that align with that belief—setting boundaries, saying no without guilt, prioritizing rest without apology. Lasting change doesn't happen by trying harder or rearranging surface habits. It happens when you get to the root. When you shift the thought patterns that are quietly driving everything.

This next section will help you do exactly that—so you can stop fighting against yourself, and finally start living from a place of deep rest and wholeness.

Let's dive in.

CHAPTER 4

Best Friend Yourself

How many of us have spent countless hours seeking validation from others, only to feel disappointed or exhausted in the end?

When I turned forty, I celebrated in a big way: hosted a dinner, took my best friends on an all-expenses-paid trip to Mexico. But when my husband asked what I wanted most for my birthday, it wasn't a lavish gift. What I truly desired wasn't the fancy dinner or the trip—it was validation. I wanted a toast. I wanted the people closest to me to take a moment to say, "You matter. You're enough." Sound narcissistic? Maybe, but it was my heart's true desire: unabashed love from those I love.

Can you relate to the longing for validation? That insatiable need to hear, "You're important, you matter, you're enough?" We all crave this. I even coached a client on it today—she'd hit a milestone in her business, yet still wished for someone to tell her it was enough. But here's the catch: sometimes, those we look to for validation are too caught up in their own worlds to offer it. And worse, they may misunderstand us or even pull back entirely, leaving us feeling rejected.

This is where rest becomes essential. When we keep seeking validation externally, we're giving away our power and energy. It's exhausting. For example, one of my clients reached out after feeling disappointed that her friends didn't celebrate good news about her health. She had hoped for a spontaneous dinner out, but instead, everyone was too busy. It stung. It felt like rejection.

I've been there. I love people and value relationships deeply. But beneath that, there's a shadow part of me that doubts my worth and seeks validation from others. This is the part that makes me perform for love and avoid rest. Does it sound familiar?

Here's the twist—at my 40th birthday dinner, one friend didn't give me a toast. Everyone else did. Her silence hurt. Even though I knew she cared, her choice felt like a rejection, a reminder that we can't control others' actions or affirmations.

And that's when it hit me: the part of me that seeks validation is at war with rest. If I'm always looking for external confirmation of my worth, I'm never truly at peace with myself. But what if there was another way to rest, a way to know our value without needing others to tell us? This is where self-compassion comes in.

According to the self-compassion researcher and professor Kristin Neff, when we struggle with the desire for validation, we can find peace and rest by learning to give ourselves the love and affirmation we seek from others. As she observes, "The beauty of self-compassion is that instead of replacing negative feelings with positive ones, new positive emotions are generated by embracing the negative ones."

Is Self-Love Selfish?

Growing up in the Christian faith, I was taught that the most important thing, the greatest commandment, was to love God and to love others. This was repeated to me over and over again and sounded like a noble way to live, whether you believe in God or not. Who can argue with loving others as a way of life?

But what's missing from the conversation, and even omitted from the verses in the Bible this idea was taken from, is the concept of loving and building a relationship with yourself: "Love your neighbour *as you love yourself.*" Even writing it now, there is a part of me that worries that loving myself is selfish and not as important as loving others. Whether you grew up with a faith background or not, our culture often teaches us that loving and serving others is the ultimate goal. But self-compassion—learning to love ourselves—is just as vital for emotional well-being and rest. Why is it that so many of us believe loving ourselves is selfish rather than essential?

Even though I was brought up to believe that God loves me, I felt so unworthy for so many years. Why did I feel like I had to perform for love—both His and others if I was so loved?

One day, I asked God, "If you think I'm so worthy of love, why don't I feel worthy?" The reply I heard, though not audibly, was clear: "It's not enough for me to think you're worthy of love, Heather. You have to agree with me."

This was a huge ah-ha moment for me—perhaps one of the top ten of my life so far. This one sentence highlighted the importance of self-acceptance and recognizing my own inherent worth. Embracing self-love is not selfish; it's essential for our emotional well-being and aligns with the commandment to love others as we love ourselves. Our agreement with our worth is what empowers us to actually feel worthy!

This is where self-compassion transforms our relationship with ourselves. Kristen Neff emphasizes that we must be kind to ourselves and accept our worth as we are, not based on what we achieve or how others see us. This is the shift we all need: *to agree we are worthy, just as we are.* When we learn to agree with our own worth, it's a powerful form of self-compassion that helps us to stop performing for love and validation. What we give our agreement to, we give our power to. So many of us have been agreeing that our value is measured by how much we can love and serve others, rather than that we are worthy simply because we exist.

Instead of prioritizing a relationship with ourselves, we've primarily focused on building relationships where we love and serve others, sometimes at the cost of ourselves. We live in a culture that celebrates when women martyr themselves, saying things like "she gave everything for her children" or "she worked tirelessly for that cause." Because we never learned how to love ourselves and give ourselves the validation we need, we are often willing to do almost anything to get that love and validation from others.

What is the antidote to the disease of self-denial at any cost that robs us from rest?

The answer is building a relationship of love and trust with yourself. Or, as I like to say to my coaching clients, learning to "best friend yourself."

Best Friend Yourself

What does best friending yourself actually look like? Is this just another thing to add to our never-ending to-do lists? Best friending yourself means treating yourself with the same compassion and kindness you'd offer a dear friend. It's about recognizing that your worth isn't based on external approval, but rather an inherent part of who you are. Best friending yourself looks like giving yourself the love, attention, and validation you want from everyone else. Instead of waiting for someone else to acknowledge your hard work, thank yourself first. Instead of looking for approval from those with more authority than you, compliment yourself.

I had my first real experience with this a few years ago on Mother's Day. It was in the middle of the pandemic and I was attempting (and failing miserably) to homeschool two kids and raise a busy toddler. I was desperate for connection, but unable to spend time with my own parents. Those were dark days, weren't they?

What I did have access to, even then, was my friendship with myself. So instead of sitting around wishing for my husband to go out and get me the perfect gift on behalf of our kids, or the kids to shower me with praise and gratitude for all the hard work I was doing, I decided to take matters into my own hands. I ordered myself a beautiful necklace, took myself out to the DQ drive-thru, and parked down the road from my house. I sat in silence on a sunny May afternoon, enjoying my Blizzard in silence. And then I proceeded to thank myself for all the little and big ways I was showing up as a mom.

"Heather, thank you for taking care of those three kids with so much love and patience. It's been a hard year, but you've continued to show up and find ways to bring fun and adventure into their lives. Thank you for all the things you do that no one else sees. Thank you for doing it all without complaining or expecting anything in return. You are an amazing mother. Well done, you."

It sounds silly to write it out here, but you know what? It felt amazing! Self-compassion teaches us that validation from others will never be enough, because it's never sustainable. But love and validation from yourself? That's endless. We often think that the validation from others will feel so much better than the validation we give to ourselves, but it's not true. Validation from others is never enough. As soon as we get some, we always want more. It feels good for a moment and then the moment passes and we are back to performing and people-pleasing in hopes of getting our next hit.

But you know what doesn't run out? Love and validation from your own darn self. You don't have to perform for it. You don't have to abandon yourself to people-pleasing to get it. And you have access to it whenever you want or need it.

Research backs this up as well. Studies show that while external validation can offer short-term boosts to self-esteem, it is ultimately unfulfilling in the long run. A study shared in *Psychological Inquiry* highlights that relying on external sources (other people's opinions) for self-worth can lead to emotional dependence, insecurity, and a lack of personal fulfillment. External validation may feel good temporarily, but without internal validation, it fails to sustain genuine well-being. Not only that, but when we base our sense of worth on external approval, we are more likely to experience anxiety, stress, and low self-esteem.

On the other hand, cultivating internal validation—where we learn to affirm and value ourselves regardless of others' opinions—has been shown to promote greater emotional resilience and mental health. An article published in 2022 reviewing multiple studies concluded that self-compassion was an important tool to "promote psychological and physiological well-being, as well as a possible prevention strategy to preserve mental and physiological health."

Becoming your own best friend is one of the best ways to connect with rest because it's sustainable. If you are tired of hustling for people's approval and validation, I'm here to tell you there is another way. And I know it feels scary to let go of that because for so long it's been the way you've made sure you were safe, loved, and that you belonged. But if you truly want to live a more rested life, the people-pleasing can't come with you.

This doesn't mean that we don't need people. We all need relationships to stay healthy and regulated. But when we learn to take care of our own needs before trying to take care of everyone else, or look for them to take care of us, our relationships become so much more fulfilling. Instead of coming to each other as black holes of need, we come full, whole, and with something to give and receive. It becomes about connection instead of co-dependency and reciprocity instead of transactional relationships. We come to our friendships to be seen, known, and loved, not to try to fill some hole that can't be filled by anyone but ourselves.

Are you ready to let go of constantly seeking approval and validation from everyone else? It won't be easy. But it will be worth it. When you begin to practice self-compassion, you reclaim your time, energy, and peace, and free yourself from the relentless cycle of people-pleasing. Just think of all the time and energy you'd get back if you stopped worrying about what other people thought and focused on how you could love yourself better?

Letting Go

The biggest time waster isn't scrolling social media, it's trying to control what other people think and how other people feel. I'm going to tell you something that you might not like or agree with about other people and their thoughts and feelings. Other people's thoughts and feelings are not your responsibility. Your decision to rest or not cannot *make* anyone think or feel anything. You can't disappoint someone. What creates feelings in other people is their own thoughts, not your actions. If you can embrace this, it will set you free from the fear of judgment. It will allow you to live a more authentic life—a life that feels restful not because of the number of naps you're taking, but because you are no longer under the weight of other people's thoughts and feelings.

It's time to start showing up as our authentic selves—to rest when we want to rest, and not worry about what other people might think. I know it's hard, especially when we see other people prioritizing work over rest. It's natural to fear they might judge us. Or when someone we love makes a comment about the rest we are taking, like "must be nice" or "when I was at that stage I never took a day to myself." But if we can let people have their thoughts and feelings and not make it mean something about us, we will be free to live a life driven by our values.

One of the most profound shifts I made in my life was learning to embrace radical acceptance. Tara Brach puts it perfectly: "Radical acceptance is the willingness to experience ourselves and our lives as they are." When we can fully accept where we are—not needing to hustle or constantly be striving for the approval of others—we can begin to experience the peace and rest that is already available to us.

If you radically accepted yourself and didn't fear the judgment of other people, what would you do differently? Would you rest more? Would you take more time for yourself? What would that feel like? Take a few minutes to journal your answers, or take yourself on a solo date and say (yes, out loud!) just how incredible you truly are.

F*** the Shoulds

We often internalize these external pressures and unconsciously believe we *should* always be doing something productive. We start "should-ing" ourselves instead of really tapping into our intuition and true desires. This might sound like, "I *should* make a meal from scratch," "I *should* keep working until this is finished" or "I *should* say yes to helping that friend even though I'm exhausted."

My relationship with rest changed dramatically when I finally started something I call "F*** the Shoulds." It was the result of a conversation my husband and I had when I was recovering from burnout. If he noticed me saying, *"I should...,"* he'd call it out and question it. Why was I putting pressure on myself to do something? Was it because I *wanted* to do that thing, or because I felt like I s*hould*? If it was a *should*, it was a no, or an opportunity to reframe what I was choosing to do and why. Instead of "I should go for a walk," I'd say, "I want to go for a walk." This simple shift helped me move away from performing for other people and their approval to tapping into my true desires and best friending myself.

If you want to get free from the shoulds, it's time to start trusting that your deepest, truest desires are actually good. So many of us believe that if we only do things because we want to, we'll live selfish lives that don't serve anyone. But what I've found to be true is the opposite of that. When I stop "shoulding" myself and actually tap in to what I want, my desires lead to good things. I want to take care of my body. I want to eat nourishing food. I want to go to bed early. I want to spend time with my children and connect with my partner. I want to serve my community and give back to causes close to my heart. But I can only discover those desires if I eliminate the shoulds. Should is about doing something out of obligation and desires is about doing something out of love.

I did an experiment a few years ago, where I decided I would take a whole week and only do what I wanted to do. No obligation, no shoulds. I was scared. I was scared that all I'd want to do all week was lay in bed and read. On the first day of the experiment my daughter came into my room and asked if I wanted to play dolls with her. I said no and felt immediate shame for being a "bad mom." But after I let that initial feeling pass, I asked myself, "What do I want to do with her?" The answer came to me quickly. "How about we go for a bike ride?" I asked. A smile lit up her face, "yes! Let's go!" Turns out I do want to spend time with my daughter, I just don't want to play with dolls with her. And that's okay. There is no *should* that's more powerful than the true desires of your heart. And you won't find them if you keep *should*-ing yourself.

Learning to rest isn't just about taking breaks—it's about setting boundaries that honour your values. For many of us, this means learning to say no. Saying no can feel incredibly difficult, especially if you've been conditioned to prioritize others' needs and expectations over your own. But saying no is one of the most powerful ways to protect your energy and live in alignment with your values.

I like to think of decisions as flowing from two different sources: 'Shoulds' and 'Wants'. Decisions rooted in 'Shoulds' often stem from obligation or guilt. They drain our energy and lead us further from our true desires. In contrast, decisions rooted in 'Wants' come from a place of alignment with our values and priorities. These are the yeses that fuel us. The key to living a more rested life is learning to separate the 'Shoulds' from the 'Wants' and to say no to the former.

- **Shoulds** → **Obligation** → **No**
- **Wants** → **Values** → **Yes**

This simple framework will help you pause and reflect before committing to something. Ask yourself: Am I saying yes because I feel obligated, or because this aligns with my values? When you begin to say no to obligations that drain you, you create space for the yeses that truly matter. Boundaries are not just about what you keep out but about what you make room for—your rest, your joy, your values.

How often do you find yourself "should-ing" yourself? Are you ready to join me in F***-ing the shoulds? Are you ready to find out what you really want and live in alignment with that?

CHAPTER 5

Rest for Your Body

When I first found the tools I use in my life coaching practice, they changed my whole life. One tool that initially impacted me and my ability to create a lifestyle of rest was based on a type of therapy called Cognitive Behavioural Therapy (CBT). CBT outlines that our thoughts create our feelings and our feelings motivate our actions so if we want to change our actions, we need to address our thoughts. This realization was so powerful for me because I'd spent most of my life experiencing my emotions as being out of my control. When I felt something, the feeling nearly always took over, and I didn't know how to stop it or control it. I resorted to either shutting my emotions down completely, which I wasn't very good at, or letting them totally run the show. Neither helped me create the lifestyle of rest I was longing for.

Do you ever feel like your emotions are taking over? I'm guessing you might because I tend to attract heart-centred women who care deeply about other people. Connection is our jam and emotions are both our superpower and our weakness, am I right?

For those of us who tend to lead with the heart, discovering that our thoughts create our feelings can give us our power back. Because even though we can't always choose our feelings, we can choose our thoughts! We are going to explore how we can process our thoughts and feelings in the next two chapters, and how they can help us access more rest in our lives. But to really lay the foundation for that conversation, we have to first talk about the autonomic nervous system and the basics of Polyvagal Theory.

First of all, what on earth is the autonomic nervous system and why does it matter? In *The Human Body in Health and Disease*, the autonomic nervous system is defined as part "of the peripheral nervous system that regulates involuntary physiologic processes including heart rate, blood pressure, respiration, digestion, and sexual arousal." The key word here is "involuntary." What this definition highlights is that even though we can choose our thoughts and those thoughts produce feelings, before all of that our autonomic nervous system is setting the stage for the quality of thoughts we are thinking. If we truly want to experience rest—body, mind, and heart—we need a nervous system that is at rest.

Many of the tools we need to understand how our nervous system works and why it matters in creating a rest-filled life, are found in Polyvagal Theory. This theory, created by psychologist Stephen Porges, helps us understand how our body and brain work together to respond to stressors that are a part of everyday life as well as experiences that are more significant, such as trauma.

To explain all of Polyvagal Theory and its implication would take an entire book and ain't nobody got time for that. If you did, you probably never would have picked up a book about rest. Instead, I'm going to highlight the parts of this theory that most pertain to our conversation about rest. Basically I've done the heavy lifting for you. And if you're interested in exploring the topic more, I highly recommend reading the book, *Anchored*, by Deb Dana.

The main thing to understand about your nervous system is that there are three states it produces:

1. *Safety* - Rest and Digest
2. *Mobilization* - Fight or Flight
3. *Immobilization* - Freeze or Shutdown

The state of safety (and rest!) is called our parasympathetic nervous system and the states of mobilization and immobilization are parts of our sympathetic nervous system. What this shows us about rest is that there is actually a good reason rest doesn't always feel accessible to us.

When our autonomic nervous system is triggered into mobilization or immobilization, we can't simply think, "I need to chill out" and then chill out. It's almost like our bodies take over and we are just hanging on for the ride. Have you ever experienced this? I'm sure you have. Maybe you're having an ordinary day and you open up your phone and see a group of your girlfriends all hanging out without you. Suddenly your heart starts racing, your hands start sweating, and you can't remember what you are supposed to be doing. Or perhaps you are making dinner and your kids start yelling at and pushing each other. All chill is lost and you immediately jump into action, yelling at them to "stop it right now." In these moments our bodies seem to have a mind of their own that can't be reasoned with.

In order to experience rest in our bodies, we need to learn how to *regulate* our autonomic nervous system, and come back to a state of safety when we get triggered. Before we dive into how we can do this, I want to remind you that the goal here is not to stay calm all the time. The goal isn't to never be triggered. That simply isn't possible. The goal is to learn how to come back home to ourselves and to a place of rest and digest, even when we are triggered. Let's talk about how to do that.

There are so many ways that you can come back to yourself, or regulate your autonomic nervous system. Instead of an exhaustive list, here is one simple way I want to share with you. The reason I'm giving you this tool specifically is because if I give you ten ways, you may not do any of them. You're already so busy you barely have time to read this book! But this one tool is so simple and it takes less than 30 seconds to apply. It can be done while you're making dinner, cleaning the house, or even going to the bathroom. Okay, here it is.

The Long Exhale

One of the easiest ways to regulate your nervous system is to make your exhale longer than your inhale. This simple breathing technique activates the parasympathetic nervous system, which promotes relaxation and helps calm your body and mind. An article in *Psychology Today* explains that extending your exhalation stimulates the vagus nerve, which can lower your heart rate and blood pressure, leaving you feeling more grounded and at ease. By practising this regularly, you can train your nervous system to respond to stress in a healthier way. If you notice yourself getting triggered—feeling like you are in fight, flight, or freeze mode—try this. Take a deep breath in through your nose for a count of three and then a slow exhale out your mouth for a count of four. Try it right now. Inhale for three, two, one, and exhale for four, three, two, one. I like to do this a few times in a row and increase the inhale to four, exhale to five, inhale to five, and exhale to six.

What does this kind of breathing do for your autonomic nervous system? When we take a longer exhale than inhale, it stimulates the vagus nerve to send a signal to our brain, activating the parasympathetic (rest and digest) nervous system and easing the sympathetic nervous system. Making your exhale longer than your inhale is *so* much more effective than just telling yourself to calm down. In fact, trying to calm yourself down by *thinking more thoughts* usually just makes it worse.

The reason why is that our state—safe or triggered, regulated or unregulated—directly affects our thoughts. Another way of saying it is that our state affects our story. When we are in our sympathetic nervous system, our prefrontal cortex or our logical brain goes offline and the quality of our thoughts decreases, creating more difficult emotions.

But when we come back to a state of safety or regulation, our prefrontal cortex comes back online. We regain our ability to observe our thoughts, decide if they are serving us or not, and change them accordingly.

We can't just think our way into rest. But we can breathe our way back to it. Isn't that a beautiful thought? The way to create rest isn't by doing more. It's not a long list of impossible tasks. It's as simple as breathing. It's accessible to you all the time. And it doesn't cost a dime.

Here are some other things you can do to regulate your autonomic nervous system when you are feeling triggered into fight, flight, or freeze:

- deep-breathing
- meditation (I recommend the Headspace app)
- stare at the horizon
- cold plunge
- laugh, cry, or scream
- dance or move intuitively
- co-regulate by connecting with a safe person
- get up and move around
- use a weighted blanket
- get into nature

I hope you don't look at this list and immediately feel overwhelmed. I know your life is full and it's hard to imagine taking time to stare at the horizon. Especially if you have a few little ones at home, this may not be the season for long walks and quiet moments. But you always have your breath. Even when your toddler is hanging off your leg as you stand at the stove preparing dinner, you can close your eyes, and breathe in for three and out for four. This alone will help you feel more rested without anything changing externally. I promise if you try it, it will help.

This past year I worked with a client who we'll call Jane. Jane came to me because she was feeling anxious and overwhelmed as a stay at home mom. Her mind was constantly imagining the worst-case scenario, especially surrounding the safety of her children.

Jane explained some of the fears she had. Fears like someone breaking into her house and night and harming or taking her children. She was nervous to leave them at daycare thinking of what might happen if a shooter entered the building. She admitted, "I know logically it's so unlikely that any of these scenarios will actually happen, but I can't seem to stop imagining it."

As I listened to her, I immediately had a sense that this wasn't a mindset issue. This was the result of dysregulation in her nervous system. So I taught her about the long exhale. It was her only homework. I didn't tell her to stop imagining the worst-case scenario or start thinking "my kids are safe." None of that would reach her if she was in her sympathetic state. I simply told her the next time she felt this way to try taking a longer exhale than inhale for a few minutes and see what happens.

The next week she came to the call excited. "Heather, you'd be so proud of me. I tried the breathing exercise and it worked. Instead of trying to convince myself my thoughts were crazy, I just paused to breathe. Nothing changed externally, but I felt so much better."

Rest starts with regulating our nervous system. It is the first step we can take to create a more rested life. And surprisingly, this approach to rest can also deeply impact our professional lives as well. Let me tell you one more story to illustrate this.

Natalie had always been driven, ambitious, and passionate about her business. But when she hired me as her business coach, she was facing the aftermath of a traumatic event in her life. This experience left her feeling overwhelmed, drained, and uncertain about the future. She had always prided herself on her ability to push through challenges, but after this event, she realized that her old way of running her business wasn't sustainable. It wasn't just her business that needed a shift—it was her entire approach to life and work.

As the primary breadwinner of her household, Natalie also carried a heavy burden of financial pressure. She was working long hours, trying to keep up with the demands of her business, and yet, it seemed like the harder she worked, the more drained and disconnected she became. She was stuck in a cycle of hustle and burnout, and her nervous system was in a constant state of fight-or-flight, leading to emotional exhaustion and a lack of clarity.

When we started working together, I introduced Natalie to nervous system regulation techniques to help her manage the stress and overwhelm that had become part of her daily life. We focused on practices like deep-breathing and grounding exercises to help her reconnect with her body and emotions. I also guided her through mindfulness and body awareness techniques to help her create a more balanced, calmer, and more energized state of being.

As Natalie began to implement these practices, she noticed immediate changes in how she felt. She started using deep-breathing exercises throughout the day, especially before making important decisions or engaging in marketing and business strategy. She found that when she took the time to pause and check in with her body and emotions, she felt more grounded and able to approach her work with clarity and confidence.

But the transformation didn't stop with nervous system regulation. We also dove deep into her business strategies. We reviewed her marketing efforts and found that much of what she was doing didn't align with her strengths or bring her joy. By identifying the strategies that felt natural and fun for her—those that made her feel authentically connected to her business—we were able to streamline her marketing approach. We built a strategy that not only resonated with her energy but also aligned with her values.

The results of this work were profound. Within months, Natalie's income increased by 40%. But what was even more exciting was that her work hours decreased, and she no longer felt the constant pressure to hustle. By building a business that respected her nervous system and emotional well-being, Natalie found herself with more energy, focus, and passion for her work than she had in years.

The best part? She felt calm and centered in her business again. The excitement and passion she had once felt but lost along the way returned. She was no longer working to exhaustion or feeling emotionally drained. Instead, she was creating a sustainable business that not only generated income but allowed her to thrive in her life.

Natalie's transformation wasn't just about increasing her revenue; it was about reclaiming her sense of peace, balance, and excitement in both her personal life and her business. She had learned to take action while staying emotionally safe, creating a sustainable pace that aligned with her body and emotions. By incorporating nervous system regulation and focusing on what truly worked for her, she was able to build a business that felt good—and one that would continue to grow.

In Natalie's words, "I hired Heather as my business coach right after experiencing a traumatic event in my life. The old way I was running my business was not sustainable for me and my nervous system. I felt a lot of pressure being the breadwinner of my home. Heather taught me how to build my business without the hustle, and with being in tune with my body and emotions. She helped me take action while still feeling emotionally safe."

Natalie's success is a testament to the power of nervous system regulation. By leaning into her strengths, embracing strategies that felt good, and honouring her body's needs, she not only grew her business but also created the space to experience more peace and joy in her work and life.

CHAPTER 6

Rest for Your Mind

Now that we are starting to understand how our nervous system affects our thoughts, let's talk about the part mindset actually plays in creating a lifestyle of rest.

Picture your mind like a garden and the thoughts you think, like the seeds you plant. Each seed, the ones you tend and the ones you don't, will inevitably grow. In the same way, our mind is full of thoughts—around sixty thousand of them a day! We notice some of them, but about 80% of them we aren't even consciously aware of. And every thought we think eventually produces fruit, or a result, in our lives. Either the fruit of rest, peace, and calm, or the fruit of stress, anxiety, and overwhelm. How do we make sure we're planting and nurturing the thoughts that create more rest in our lives?

I tried planting a little garden last summer in the two raised garden boxes tucked in a sunny corner of our front yard. We filled them with fresh soil, and one sunny day in May, my youngest son and I planted the seeds. It was all going so well at first. Little rows scattered with tiny seeds, watered almost daily, and baked in the summer sun. But half of the garden didn't grow. The tomatoes and cucumbers in particular, never produced fruit. Not one piece. We later discovered that some of the seeds we planted were old or not great quality (avoid grocery store tomato plant seeds, okay?). Turns out the quality of the seeds you plant actually affects how fruitful the garden will be.

When we imagine tending to the garden of our mind, the quality of our thoughts matters. But instead of focusing on *not thinking* certain thoughts, we gain more traction by focusing on replacing the negative thoughts with *powerful thoughts*. When we focus more on what we want, rather than on what we *don't* want, change happens faster. Why is this? Because where our attention goes, our energy flows. What we look for, we find. This is just how the brain works. But we'll explore more about that later.

Back to your thoughts. You may have noticed I said replacing negative thoughts with *powerful* thoughts, not positive ones. The key to unlocking the potential of your beautiful brain to create a more rested life is to understand the difference between positive thoughts and powerful thoughts.

What is the difference between these two kinds of thoughts, and why does one create a lifestyle of rest and one leaves us feeling like we are always falling short?

The difference is belief.

In order for a thought to be powerful, we need to believe it, even just a little bit. This is why looking in the mirror and saying "I'm a rested woman" doesn't work. Because we don't believe it! We hear the thought and our brains immediately call BS on it.

I'm definitely *not* always a rested woman. I'm often the woman who is running from one kid's class to another one's game. The woman who is standing over the freezer wondering if chicken fingers twice in one week is too much. The woman who forgets her sons' dentist appointment and hasn't booked one for herself in several years.

Rewiring our brain for rest isn't about applying toxic positivity, where we deny our feelings and gaslight ourselves, in hopes of feeling better fast. If that worked I would teach you that instead. But it doesn't work. In order for a thought to be effective, we have to actually believe it. And the way we know if we believe it or not is how it feels in our body when we think it.

I like to think of thoughts on a scale from -10 to +10. Your current thought about rest might be something like "I don't have time for rest." Let's call that a -7 thought on the belief scale. To expect yourself to jump from a -7 thought to a +10 thought overnight isn't realistic. But what if you could move from a -7 to a +1 or 2 and continue to build up to a 8 or 9 over time? This is what building powerful thoughts is all about. The smallest shift can take a positive thought and make it a powerful one, and lead to a deeper experience of rest in your life.

The Rest Belief Scale

Negative Thoughts				Neutral			Powerful thoughts	
-10	-7	-5	-2	0	+2	+5	+8	+10
Rest is lazy	I don't have time	Rest is a waste of time	I can't afford to rest	Maybe I can rest	I can rest a little	Rest helps me	Rest is essential	Rest is sacred

The Shift

The shift comes in the form of two little phrases: "I'm learning" and "It's possible." Take any positive thought you've been trying to believe, add one of these phrases to the beginning, and see what happens in your body when you think it.

Instead of thinking, "I'm a rested woman," try "I'm learning to become a rested woman." Or "It's possible I could be more rested than I am." Do you see how that feels different in your body? The difference you feel is the difference belief makes.

The way to know if the thought is powerful for you is to try it out, and see how it feels when you say it. Does it feel like shame? It's not going to work. Does it feel like discouragement? Also not the best fuel for transformation.

But maybe it feels like curiosity or possibility or even certainty. Those are the emotions that fuel us to take the small, repeated actions, over time, that create lasting transformation in our lives.

Do you think this approach seems too gentle? Maybe even a little soft. Don't we need to will power and white knuckle our way into change?

Not if you want the change to be lasting.

Using shame and coercion with ourselves is exactly the opposite of how we create a more rested life, because it breaks down the fabric of our relationship with ourselves. And building self-trust *is* the way to create rest. We need to be gentle in our approach, which is why the tone of the words we speak to ourselves matters as much as the words themselves.

In a study by Kelly Werner and colleagues, participants were asked to write about a personal failure or mistake. They were split into two groups: one group was instructed to write about the event with a tone of self-criticism, while the other group wrote about the same event but with a focus on self-compassion, imagining they were comforting a friend who had experienced the same situation. Those in the self-compassion group reported feeling less shame and more motivated to make positive changes after the exercise. In contrast, the self-critical group felt demoralized and stuck, with little desire to take constructive action. This perfectly illustrates how approaching our mistakes with gentleness and understanding fosters self-trust and growth, whereas shame breaks down our inner resilience and prevents progress.

Your Rest Thoughts

When you think about rest, what are the main beliefs that come up? Take a moment to pull out your journal or the notes in your phone and write down all of your thoughts about rest.

The way you are currently thinking about rest is directly linked to how rested you feel.

Here are some the common thoughts I hear women say about rest:

"I feel guilty resting."

"I need to be productive before I can let myself rest."

"I don't have time to rest."

"I don't deserve rest."

"If I rest, other people around me will suffer."

These thoughts are a big part of the reason we aren't very rested. It isn't our busy schedule, our many children and their requests, the emails from the school, and the never-ending pile of laundry on our couch. All of these things are neutral. There may be something in you that resists believing that, but stay with me. This is the pathway to your freedom.

The circumstances of your life are powerless until you have a thought about them. What makes you feel stressed, overwhelmed, anxious, and exhausted is the story you're telling yourself about your circumstances.

This is good news and bad news. The bad news is you *have* to do something about it. The good news is you *can* do something about it.

You are a lot more powerful in your life than you give yourself credit for. Life is not happening to you. You are an active participant and it all starts in the garden of your mind. If you want to stop feeling so burnt out, it's time to stop thinking, "I don't have time to rest." You have time for what you make time for. I know I'm being firm with you. But I promise it's because I love you. I was where you are just a few years ago and this truth is what set me free. If you want to change your life, you need change your thoughts.

Instead of telling yourself that rest just isn't possible for you, try one of these out:

"I am worthy of rest."

"Rest is productive."

"I have time for what matters most to me."

Which one feels powerful to you? Which one moves you to want to show up in a different way in your life? Which one do you believe, even just a bit? That is your powerful thought.

63 Days

Once you've found a powerful thought about rest by shifting your language and tone, the next step is to give it time. Just like when you plant a tiny lettuce seed in the ground, you aren't making a whole salad with it the next day, thoughts take time to grow and produce fruit. Neuroscientist Dr. Caroline Leaf suggests that it takes about 63 days for a brand-new thought to become a neural pathway in our brains. This means that it takes just over two months of thinking your powerful thoughts daily before it becomes your new default setting. Dr. Leaf emphasizes that while initial changes in thought patterns can begin within the first 21 days, sustaining these changes and solidifying new neural pathways require an additional 42 days, totalling 63 days. This extended period allows for the reinforcement of new thought habits, leading to more permanent behavioural changes. By consistently nurturing this thought, you're giving your brain the time it needs to form a lasting, healthy new pattern.

My favourite way to nurture these little thought-seeds is to put them as a reminder in my phone. Here are the steps to do that if you have an iPhone:

1. Go to the Reminder app
2. Hit the "+ New Reminder" button
3. Type in your powerful thought
4. Hit the "info" button
5. Add the time you want it to pop up each day
6. Click the "repeat" button and choose "Daily"

Thinking this thought, once a day, every day, for 63 days is where it all starts. We will talk about some practical action you can take to create and support a lifestyle of rest in Chapter 7, but this is where we start for now. Planting the seed. Nurturing it daily. If you really want a life of rest, this step is even easier than taking a nap.

I did this exercise with a client who was struggling to follow through with her workout plan. She'd purchased a Peloton and every time she saw it sitting unused in her office, she felt guilty. "I should be riding that bike!" "What a waste of money!" "Why am I such a procrastinator?" In our coaching session I walked her through creating a powerful thought about her Peloton. It sounded something like, "I'm so proud of myself for taking the first step in my health journey." I told her the homework for that week was NOT to get on the bike, but to practice the thought once a day.

The next week she came to the call with a huge smile on her face. She went on to tell me how after a few days of practising the thought, she actually felt motivated to get on her bike. And even though I told her NOT to ride it, she had already done three rides!

It wasn't the guilt or shame that changed her actions—it was the belief.

So often we want evidence before we are willing to believe. We want to see the number on the scale go down before we believe we can lose weight. We want the money in our account before we can believe we are wealthy. We want romantic moments with our partner before we can believe we have an awesome relationship.

But belief proceeds evidence. The belief is what creates the evidence!

And the reason this creates more rest in our life is because it keeps us from hustling and striving to make things happen before we are willing to believe. We start with belief. We start with thinking a thought, once a day, for 63 days. And that is even easier than going to the gym.

CHAPTER 7

Feel Your Feelings

When it comes to creating more rest in our lives, our thoughts are the starting line. But when considering how to *sustain* a lifestyle of rest, it's more about our heart and our emotions. In this chapter we're going to explore how learning to process and respond to *all* of our emotions is the key to creating a sustainable lifestyle of rest.

For as long as I can remember, my life was run by my emotions. I'd be going along, living my life and then suddenly—like a wave—an emotion would come and completely take over. Sometimes these emotions would even take me out for days or weeks at a time. One of the most memorable times this happened was after my first break up. I was twenty years old, and I'd been dating the guy on and off for four years. Even though the relationship was pretty unhealthy, I'd convinced myself I was going to marry the guy. When it finally ended, the emotions that came up were so overwhelming. It really felt like my life was ending.

At the time I was finishing my education degree, and every day I had to teach a rowdy group of third grade students. I remember driving to the school and crying all the way there. And it wasn't just a few tears gently rolling down my cheek.

It was uncontrollable sobbing for the entire twenty-minute drive, with tears and snot all over my face. When I arrived at the school, I'd attempt to mop up the mess on my face, and shove my feelings down, just to get through the day. This went on for weeks. So many emotions and no idea what to do with them all.

Being at the mercy of your emotions is an incredibly frustrating way to live, isn't it? It's the feeling of being totally out of control. A big part of us may even believe that something is wrong with us because of the big emotions we're experiencing? Can you relate to this?

When I wasn't feeling totally overcome with the emotions of the break up, I tried the approach of ignoring my feelings and pushing them down. Someone would ask me how I was doing and I'd say "fine", even though I knew the real answer was "not good at all." But this strategy only worked for a few minutes or hours until the emotions I'd been pushing down like a beach ball in a pool would inevitably pop up, sometimes smacking me right in the face.

When it comes to our emotions, I often think of the image of driving a car. Where are your emotions in the car right now? Are they in the driver's seat, making the decisions and determining the direction of your life? Or have you shoved them into the backseat, or even the trunk, believing they are unreliable, bad, or wrong?

So many of us treat our emotions like they are problems to be fixed. Even after five years of doing the work of building emotional health and teaching my clients to do the same, I still don't enjoy feeling sad, angry, anxious, or frustrated. There is a part of us that resists and judges negative emotion every time. Even calling them "negative" is an example of how much we dislike them. But all the energy we spend resisting and judging our uncomfortable emotions keeps us from the life of rest we desire.

If you want to create and sustain a life of rest, it's time to learn how to feel your feelings. One of my favourite quotes from psychologist Hillary McBride emphasizes this saying, "If I could sum up all my years of clinical training and research in one statement, it would be this: We heal when we can be with what we feel."

But how do you actually do that?

Here's the thing, my friend. It's simple, but it's not easy. What I'm going to attempt to do here is give you the simple steps to feel your feelings, knowing that they are often very difficult steps to take.

How to Feel a Feeling

1. **Notice.** We often become immersed in a feeling before we consciously register its presence. But if we can take a moment to notice and pay attention to it, we can slow the process right down. Awareness is the beginning of change. The next time you start feeling something, try to take a moment during or after to notice when it started. What were you doing? What did you see or hear that might have triggered it? Where did the feeling start?

Notice the feeling without judgment and with curiosity. Sometimes I use the phrase "isn't it interesting" to shift from judging to noticing. "Isn't it interesting that I feel this way right now?"

2. **Name.** The next step is to give the emotion a name. Many of us struggle to identify what we are actually feeling. We are so accustomed to giving answers like "fine" or "good" that it's hard to identify the subtleties of our emotions. One way to grow your emotional vocabulary is to use the emotion wheel. You can find a copy of the emotion wheel online and print it out for easy reference.

In a 2007 study, Dr. Matthew Lieberman and his team explored how labelling or naming emotions affects brain activity. Participants were shown emotional images designed to bring up feelings like anger, fear, or sadness, and were asked to either simply experience the emotions or label them with words, like "I feel angry" or "I feel sad." The results were striking. When participants named the emotion they were experiencing, it led to a noticeable decrease in activity in the amygdala, the brain region responsible for processing intense emotions. At the same time, the prefrontal cortex, which is involved in higher-level thinking and emotional regulation, became more active.

This study shows a simple but powerful insight: naming our emotions helps us process them more effectively. Instead of letting emotions take over and control us, labelling them engages our rational brain, allowing us to step back and manage our feelings. This shift from the emotional, reactive amygdala to the thoughtful prefrontal cortex is what helps us regulate and understand our emotions better. In essence, by simply naming our feelings, we gain more control over them and reduce their intensity.

The next time you're feeling an emotion, write it down, text a friend, or even say it out loud to yourself: "I feel sad/scared/anxious."

3. **Feel.** This may sound obvious, but it's not. Feeling our feelings is something we often try to do with our minds. But thoughts are processed in the mind, and emotions are processed *in the body*. However, we can recruit our brain to help us stay in our body by asking ourselves questions like this:

- Where do I feel this emotion in my body?
- Is it hot or cold?
- Is it moving fast or slow?
- If this feeling was a colour, what colour would it be?

The crazy thing is, we can actually process a feeling in as little as ninety seconds to five minutes, *when we don't resist it.* Crazy right? Dr. Jill Bolte Taylor, a neuroanatomist, explains that when we experience an emotion, the physiological response—triggered by a stimulus—lasts about 90 seconds in the body before it dissipates.

After this initial period, any remaining emotional response is a result of our thoughts and interpretations, not the emotion itself. By allowing ourselves to fully experience and process the emotion without resistance, we can prevent it from lingering longer than necessary.

When we resist, they persist. When we feel them, they flow through us.

4. **Ask.** Emotions are messengers. They are not the best drivers, nor are they meant to be shoved in the trunk. But they are like little "check engine" lights on the dashboard of our souls. They aren't here to destroy or sabotage us. They are here to tell us something that can help us. Take a minute to ask your emotion "what are you here to tell me?" Often what they have to say is exactly the wisdom we need to move forward.

Many of us have been told not to trust our emotions, but this messaging has caused us harm. It's caused us to ignore these important messengers who are here to help us. It's caused us to spend so much time and energy resisting our feelings instead of resting in them. If we truly want to live a lifestyle of rest, it will require us to feel our feelings, in the moment, as they come up.

In 2023, I fell down the stairs in our home, and broke my ankle. For weeks and even months after, I was often overcome with sadness whenever I thought about the experience. I was sad I couldn't work out, sad I couldn't carry a cup of coffee up the stairs, sad I couldn't cook dinner for my family. When the sadness would come, I would cry. No resistance, no judgment, just tears. And you know what? I probably only spent about 5 minutes crying each time. Even if that was 5 minutes a day for 30 days, that's only a total of 150 minutes, or just under 2 hours. The remainder of the time I spent resting and healing.

Here's the deal. I could have spent that whole first month after my accident resisting instead of resting. And all it would have done is make a hard experience even harder. That's what I did after that breakup. And the grieving process lasted *so* much longer because of it. Instead of taking a few weeks or months to process the loss of that relationship and what I thought it would be, it took me years. To be honest, it lasted over a decade without me even realizing it. The relationship ended in 2005 and then nearly fifteen years later, tragedy struck.

It was a quiet Wednesday evening, the night before my husband's birthday, and I got a text from a friend I rarely talked to.

"Did you hear the news? He's dead. He passed away in a ski accident."

The guy I'd dated for four years and cried over for months after, had passed away skiing in the mountains he loved. And I was wrecked. I hadn't seen him in nearly fifteen years, but I grieved as though we had just broken up. And I think the reason it took me so long to finally let go is because I didn't know how to feel my feelings when we first broke up. I resisted and judged them so much and as a result, never felt fully at rest in this area.

After he passed away, I let myself truly feel it. Even though it probably seemed confusing to people and was even confusing to me, I felt it. I cried, I journaled, I went to therapy. I felt without judgment or resistance. And finally, after all this time, I came to a place of rest and peace.

Where are you resisting instead of resting? What feelings are you overwhelmed by, or shutting down, that are keeping your body in fight, flight, or freeze, instead of rest and restore? What healing are you delaying because you're afraid to feel your feelings without judgment?

A gentle reminder to take a deep breath in through your nose for a count of three and then a slow exhale out your mouth for a count of four.

Friend, I know it's scary, but I want to invite you to lean into your uncomfortable emotions. To imagine them like a marshmallowy cloud in front of you and lean all the way in. I know there is a part of you that fears they will consume you; that they will swallow you whole. But I promise, you were designed to feel your feelings, not fight them.

If it feels way too scary to do this on your own, I would encourage you to find a coach, therapist or friend who can walk with you. Some feelings we can process on our own, and others just feel too big to face alone. If you don't know where to go to find this kind of help, please reach out to me! I'd love to walk with you, or point you in the direction of someone safe who can. You don't have to do this on your own.

CHAPTER 8

Living From Not For

So far we've covered how we can create more rest in our lives by attending to our body, mind, and emotions. But maybe you're still wondering, with all this resting, how are we supposed to get any work done? We still have bills to pay, goals to accomplish, and dreams to pursue. Don't worry—I've got you. Just because we are prioritizing rest doesn't mean we can't also get some shiz done!

I love crushing my to-do list as much as the next person. But what I've learned is that rest and action are not mutually exclusive. They are not in conflict with one another. In fact, when we learn to work from a rested place, we are so much more productive in our work.

A lifestyle of rest is about learning to live and work FROM instead of FOR.

What does it mean to work FROM instead of FOR?

It means we deeply understand and believe that we are worthy, valuable, and significant *before* we do a single productive thing. *Worthiness becomes our starting point instead of our end goal.*

Do you believe that you are worthy, even when you aren't productive? That you are valuable, even when you aren't contributing? It's easy to say that about someone else, but hard to truly believe it about yourself.

I had a call with a new client the other day and she was telling me about all the pressure she feels as a wife, mom of two young sons, and full-time working professional. She shared how she used to feel like she was thriving in her life and now she feels like she's barely surviving. As she described trying so hard to read all the books and take all the courses and do all the right things, she started to cry. "I just feel like none of it's enough. I feel like I'm not enough. I feel like I'm losing my light."

So many of us feel this way, don't we? Like in the face of everything that needs to be done, we are simply not enough. We don't have enough time, energy, or resources to be everything to everyone.

Just think about the last time you sat around and truly did nothing. No phone, no agenda, just you sitting still. If you can't remember a time like this, take a moment to try to imagine it. What if you did nothing for the rest of the day today? What thoughts and feelings come up for you? Guilt? Shame? Fear?

If the idea of doing nothing is uncomfortable for you, it's possible you've been living FOR instead of FROM.

Can it really be true that we are worthy of love even if we aren't doing anything at all? I can't help but think about how I felt about each of my three children when they were first born. Before they did a single thing, I loved them completely. I believed they were valuable before they took a step, said a word, cleaned up a toy, or contributed to our family in any practical way. Humans are worthy of love not because of what they do, but who they are. We are significant simply because we exist. And when we start to embrace this, it changes everything.

Let me tell you the story of what it means to live FROM instead of FOR and how it empowers us to take action from rest.

A few years ago I was having breakfast with a dear friend and our conversation changed my life. At the time, I was ten years into a career of motivational speaking and I was feeling really stuck in my efforts to grow my platform and my business. I was constantly looking for a bigger stage, a better opportunity, and the hustle of it was burning me out. As I was sharing my struggle with her, she asked me this question: "Heather, what motivates you to continue pursuing a career in speaking?"

I responded by telling her how I felt when I spoke. "Every time I'm on stage I feel so significant. When I'm sharing tools that can change lives, from the stage, it feels like my life has purpose."

Then she asked me the question that changed my life (sounds dramatic, but it really did change everything!). She asked me, "What if you already are significant, even before you get on the stage?"

Mic drop. Jaw drop.

Could it be?

What if I was already significant? What if I didn't have to work for it, earn it, achieve it, because *I already possessed it?!* What if I could stop the hustle and actually rest in that truth?

Worthiness and Significance

Worthiness and significance are often intertwined, but they focus on different aspects of how we view ourselves and our place in the world. Worthiness is the belief that we are valuable simply because we exist. It's an internal sense of being enough, even when we're not accomplishing anything or fulfilling any external role. Our worthiness is not determined by what we do, but by who we are. It's the quiet knowing that we deserve love, respect, and care, no matter our productivity or achievements. Worthiness is about resting in the truth that you are enough, just as you are.

Significance, on the other hand, relates to our impact and how we contribute to the world around us. It's the sense that we matter, that our actions have purpose, and that we are playing a meaningful role in our families, communities, and careers. Significance often comes from our relationships and the impact we feel we are making in the world. While worthiness is unconditional, significance is usually tied to the actions we take and the difference we make. But here's the shift: what if your significance is inherent (like your worthiness) and doesn't need to be earned? What if you could rest in the truth that you are significant, even before you take a single step toward achieving anything?

When we live from a place of worthiness, we stop chasing after significance to prove we matter. We begin to work from a place of rest, knowing that we are valuable whether or not we accomplish everything on our to-do list. This shift allows us to be productive without burning out, because our worth is no longer dependent on our achievements. When we embrace both our worthiness and our significance, we free ourselves from the constant pressure to perform and can work from a more rested, grounded place.

Let this thought sink in: What if *you* are already significant? What if everything that you've been working so hard for—value, worth, purpose, significance—is already yours?

My friend, today I'm here to remind you, you are already worthy *and* significant. Before you do a thing or help a single person, in big or small ways, you are already enough.

After my dear friend dropped that truth bomb, she asked me this follow up question, "If you truly believed you were already significant, what would you want to do next? Would you still want to speak on stage?"

My answer, to my own shock, was, "No."

"If I really believed I was already significant, I wouldn't need to be on the stage. If I truly knew I was significant, I'd want to help other people feel significant. And the best way I can do that is by becoming a life coach. And also, I'd have another baby."

And that's exactly what I did.

Instead of continuing to hustle for a bigger platform and more influence trying to prove my worth, I let it all go. I stopped going after bigger stages and more followers and allowed myself to rest in the truth that I was already enough. In the end, that conversation is what led me to have a third child, my son Byron, and to start my coaching business. All of it was birthed from a place of rest, the rest that comes when we start to believe that we are already enough.

When we believe that love, worthiness, or significance are destinations we must reach, the timeline becomes our focus. Rest happens when we stop striving and choose to be fully here, right now. When we believe there is a specific path, we must take to get there and timeline we must follow to earn our worthiness, rest feels like a threat to our very identity. Success becomes a destination that we are rushing to and burnout becomes inevitable.

But when we understand that love, worthiness, and significance are the *starting line*, our actions are fuelled by rest, and our potential is limitless. Success becomes so much more about the journey than the destination, and can look like so many different things. It's not about hitting a certain revenue goal, number of followers, or any other external measure. It's about knowing we are already enough and allowing our action to be fuelled from that place. When we live FROM instead of FOR, we get to ask ourselves, "now what do I want to do next?" and do it!

Living FOR Worthiness

Living FROM Worthiness

When we work FOR worthiness:

- we are in a rush
- we struggle to say no
- we resist setting healthy boundaries
- we feel guilty resting because it feels like a threat to our worthiness
- we ignore our nervous systems and emotions, thinking they will slow us down
- we work endlessly towards the goal at the cost of our health and relationships
- "success" only looks like one thing

When we work FROM worthiness:

- we aren't in a rush
- we are confident in saying yes and no
- we set healthy boundaries
- we enjoy our rest knowing we are worthy in it
- we attend to our nervous system and take time to process our emotions
- we work with diligence, while investing into our health and relationships
- success is unlimited!

Have you been living FROM love, worthiness, and significance, or FOR it? If you're feeling tired, burnt out, and done with the hustle, maybe it's time to make this shift. Maybe it's time to embrace the truth that you are already worthy. You are already loved. You are already significant. This isn't up for debate. It's not dependent on your ability to get things done. It's your birthright.

You are worthy because you are here.

If you truly believed this, what would you do next?

CHAPTER 9

Rest Is Productive

The argument many of us make for not resting is that we have so much to do and not enough time. How can we possibly justify taking time to rest when the list is so long? But what if I told you that resting, especially when you're tired, is actually more productive that pushing through and working? What if rest is actually one of the most productive things you can do?

Did you know that while you sleep, your brain is literally solving problems? During REM sleep, your brain replays newly stored information from the day and compares and connects it to your other stored memories. This process allows your brain to make connections and associations *you can't make while awake*, allowing you to see problems from a new perspective. The challenges you faced throughout the day, that you couldn't figure out, are actually being solved while you sleep! How cool is that? Maybe instead of saying, "I don't have time to sleep," we should be saying, "I don't have time *not* to sleep!"

Not only is rest productive for your mind, it's also productive for your body. When you rest, you give your muscles time to recover from their physical activity, as well as the brain and organs time to replenish their energy stores. Adequate rest is essential for maintaining overall physical health. It supports immune function, regulates hormone levels, and promotes healing and repair processes within the body. Chronic lack of rest is linked to various health problems, including cardiovascular disease, obesity, and weakened immune function.

I have lived this reality out in my own life and body. As I mentioned in Chapter 7, in 2023 I broke my ankle in the most unexciting way. It was a typical Friday morning and I was heading downstairs to get my kids ready for school. My foot slipped on the first step, sending me down four stairs where I landed on a rolled ankle. The pain was so intense I almost passed out. At first I thought maybe it was just a sprain, but after realizing I couldn't walk, I headed to the ER where the doc declared, "Looks like you broke your ankle."

Being a mom of three kids, married to a very busy husband, and the CEO of a business, taking time to heal felt absolutely impossible and completely unproductive. But the truth about healing is that our body is designed to do it. But a lot of that healing, especially at the beginning, happens when we rest, not when we work. Yes, eventually I had to do the "work" of physiotherapy to rebuild my strength, but even that was a slow and gentle process that required a lot more resting than working. While I lay in bed for weeks, seemingly "doing nothing", my body was busy working to repair a broken bone and rebuild torn and stretched tendons and ligaments. It wasn't running, jumping, and working out that healed my body. It was resting that healed me.

Rest is also productive for your emotional health. It provides an opportunity to relax, unwind, and engage in activities that bring joy and fulfillment. Regular rest can help prevent burnout, reduce feelings of overwhelm, and promote a greater sense of balance and contentment in life. You may already know this, but rest helps reduce stress levels by lowering cortisol, the body's primary stress hormone. Engaging in relaxing activities or simply taking time to rest can promote relaxation and lower overall stress levels. It's pretty amazing the healing that happens while you sleep. For example, when you are in deep sleep, the part of your brain that regulates your emotions (the amygdala) communicates with the part responsible for reason and logic (the prefrontal cortex). These connections are essential for us to regulate our emotions more effectively when we are awake, and explains why we often feel more emotional when we are sleep deprived.

It's a joke in our family that you can't talk to Mom after 10pm because she turns into a pumpkin, and it's true! Any conversation I try to have, or decision I attempt to make, never goes well that late in the day. This is why we can feel so overwhelmed by the challenges in our life right before we fall asleep, but wake up with a totally new perspective! It's because of the magic that happens while we sleep.

Contrary to the belief that constant activity leads to greater productivity, research suggests that regular breaks can actually improve efficiency and productivity. Even taking short breaks during your work day allows you to return to tasks with renewed energy and concentration, leading to better overall performance. In an *Applied Psychology* study, researchers explored how short breaks during work can enhance productivity and overall well-being. They found that taking micro-breaks created improved energy levels and reduced fatigue. Participants experienced a significant increase in focus and energy and a decrease in fatigue after taking short breaks.

A gentle reminder to take a deep breath in through your nose for a count of three and then a slow exhale out your mouth for a count of four.

I often encourage my clients to take micro-breaks from their work, rather than "pushing through", even when working on tight deadlines. For all of the reasons we just discussed, taking a break to nap, walk, meditate, or connect with someone safe is more helpful, beneficial, and productive than pushing through.

Imagine this scenario: It's Thursday evening and you have a project with the deadline of 9am Friday morning. It's 9pm and your mind and body are tired from a long day of work. You can either: (a) force yourself to stay awake, do sub-par work from 9pm-1am and get a crappy sleep from 1am-8am. Or (b) stop working at 9pm, relax for an hour, sleep from 10pm-6am and then get up early with a fresh mind and body, and get your work done from 6am-8am. Which sounds better to you? Four hours of sub par, unfocused work, or two hours of focused, creative work, from rest? If you want to increase your productivity, it's time to increase your rest.

The idea that rest is productive most deeply hit me when I was pregnant with our first child. I was home for the day because there were no substitute teaching jobs available. It was a beautiful fall day and our front yard was covered with leaves. Because I loved being productive so much, I decided to go outside and rake the yard. As someone who worked out regularly and prided myself on being able to do almost any job a man could do, I was sure I'd have the work done in no time.

But after about an hour of raking, I was exhausted. Instead of resting, I pushed myself to keep going, but eventually had to stop. I went inside to lay down for a minute and ended up sleeping for two hours.

Later that week I took a pregnancy test and found out I was expecting! Over the next 9 months I really struggled. I struggled because even though I prided myself on accomplishing a lot each day, I was tired all the time. Taking an hour or two nap each day became the norm. And one day when my husband got home from work, I cried to him about how useless and lazy I felt.

"I'm just lying around doing nothing," I said, through teary eyes.

I remember he looked straight at me and said "Babe, you're more productive than you've ever been—you're creating a life!"

This is when I first started to clue in to the fact that rest was productive. While I was lying around "doing nothing", my body was busy creating a human being. Rest gave birth to greatness!

PART 3
LIVING THE REVOLUTION

It's time to move from understanding the problem and shifting our mindset, to embracing the power of taking action. While knowing what needs to change is an important step, it's quite different from actually making those changes. Habits are hard to break, and transforming our lives requires more than just good intentions. This part of the book is about living the revolution, where the transformation becomes tangible. It's about turning what you've learned into practical, actionable steps that you can integrate into your everyday life. The benefits of this transformation aren't just short-term fixes; they are long-lasting shifts that will ripple through every area of your life. By embodying rest as a daily practice, you'll create a sustainable lifestyle that nurtures your mind, body, and soul, allowing you to thrive in a way that isn't defined by hustle, but by true, holistic well-being.

Before we dive into these practical steps, let's take a moment to assess where your relationship with rest is at currently. A Rest Audit will give you a clear picture of your current rest patterns and help you identify where adjustments are needed. This simple exercise will provide you with insight into how much rest you're truly getting, how you're prioritizing it, and where you can make shifts to support a more balanced, restful lifestyle. Completing this audit will help you build a strong foundation for the changes you're about to make.

A Rest Audit

Taking time to rest often feels harder than we think it will. That's why we resist it, postpone it, or fill our moments with distractions. To understand how you relate to rest, let's start with a simple exercise: a Rest Audit. In order to do this exercise, you'll need some paper and a pen. Maybe even break into that stash of pretty journals you've been saving for the right moment.

Step 1: Reflect on Your Week

Think about the past week. Identify one moment each day (if applicable) when you resisted rest. These could be times when:

- You felt tired but kept working instead of taking a break.
- You chose to scroll through your phone instead of sitting quietly.
- You noticed an opportunity to rest but felt guilty or anxious about taking it.

Step 2: Write Down the Details

For each moment, answer the following:

1. What was happening? Describe the situation.
2. What did you feel? Note any emotions (e.g., guilt, anxiety, frustration).
3. What did you do instead of resting? Identify the action you took to avoid rest.

Step 3: Explore the Why

For each moment, ask yourself:

- Why did I resist rest?
    - Did I feel I didn't deserve it?
    - Was I afraid of falling behind?
    - Did I feel pressured to stay busy or productive?
- What would have happened if I had rested?

Step 4: Recognize Patterns

After completing your audit, look for common themes. Do you often avoid rest for similar reasons (e.g., guilt, external expectations, or fear of being unproductive)? Recognizing these patterns is the first step toward breaking the cycle.

Here's what these first four steps could look like in your journal:

When You Resisted Rest	What was happening?	Emotion	"Instead of resting I…"	Why?	Patterns
ex. Saturday afternoon	Kids were playing, house was messy	Guilt, anxiety	Cleaned the kitchen instead of sitting with a book	Felt like I "should" be productive, but I also knew I was exhausted	Tendency to prioritize productivity over rest

Step 5: Set an Intention

Based on your reflections, set one simple intention for the week ahead. I would encourage you to only pick one and practice it for at least a month before adding another one. Here are a few examples:

- "I will take one 10-minute break every afternoon to sit quietly."
- "I will pause for 5 minutes before saying yes to any new commitment."

By taking the time to complete this Rest Audit, I hope you gain valuable insight into your current relationship with rest and the barriers that may be holding you back. Awareness is the first step toward change. As you move forward in this chapter, use these reflections to create intentional shifts—ones that will help you embrace rest not as a luxury, but as a vital part of a thriving, sustainable life.

CHAPTER 10

Values, Goals, and Scheduling

If you want to embrace a lifestyle of rest while still living out your purpose, it's essential to learn the skill of time mastery. Time is one of our most valuable resources especially because it is limited. We each have 24 hours a day, but we don't know how many days we have. We do, however, know that our days are limited. The average person lives to be 85 years old giving us all about 4420 weeks to live. By the time you're reading this book, you are likely 30-40 years old, giving you 2300-2800 weeks of life left to live. It doesn't sound like a whole lot when put that way, does it?

I don't tell you that to freak you out or create a sense of time scarcity. I tell you that to remind you how precious your time truly is. If you want to invest your time in a way that is purposeful, intention and led by rest, understanding what your values are is the first step.

Your values are the guiding force that shapes what truly matters to you—what you want to prioritize and where you want to focus your energy. Once you have clarity on your values, your goals will serve as the roadmap to help you live in alignment with those values. But even the best intentions and goals are only as good as your ability to execute them in the real world. This is where your schedule comes in. A well-structured schedule ensures that your daily actions are in alignment with your values and goals, allowing you to create space for rest, play, and work without compromise. It's this flow—values, goals, and schedule—that creates an opportunity for true transformation to happen. By intentionally building your schedule around what matters most to you, you can begin to create a life where rest is not a luxury, but a priority.

Your Core Values

What are your personal core values? What are the deeply ingrained principles that guide your decisions and help you craft a meaningful life? If you don't immediately know your answer to that question, don't worry. You're not alone. But understanding and defining those values is key to living a life led by rest, rather than hustle. When you know your values, making decisions about how to invest your time is so much easier.

Let's spend some time defining your core values. I go through this exercise in more depth in my coaching membership CEO Flow, which you can learn more about at heatherboersma.com. In the meantime, here are some questions to consider when defining your values. Write down your answers to these questions as you're going through them.

1. How do you want to be remembered? What words do you want people to use to define how you lived your life?
2. Who is someone you deeply admire and why? What do they prioritize that draws you to them?

3. When you're seventy, what do you imagine you'll be most proud of yourself for? What would you wish you did more of or less of?

My personal core values in this season of my life are connection, adventure, and impact. These three words have been my north star for the past five years. They have guided my decisions both in my business and my personal life. These values are a big reason we moved our family of five across the country from Winnipeg to Vancouver. When we first entertained the idea of moving, I questioned if it was the right decision. I felt like people only moved if it was for work or some kind of calling from God. For us it was neither of those things. It was a decision led by our value for adventure. We wanted to create a life where we could ski and hike and explore as a family. And though we could do some of those things living where we were, we could integrate that value easier in Vancouver. So we moved. We made a decision about how to invest our time, money, and energy based on our values. It wasn't the easiest decision, and it cost us something (um hello most expensive city in Canada), but the cost is worth it because it aligns with our values.

After you've defined your values, the next step in time mastery is creating goals that are aligned with those values.

Values-Based Goal-Setting

Traditional goal-setting is often built around productivity, achievement, and the pursuit of more. Hustle culture tells us to dream big, push harder, and never stop striving. But where does that leave us? Exhausted, overwhelmed, and sometimes disconnected from the very things that matter most—our values. I've been there—setting ambitious goals, hitting milestones, and still feeling like something was missing. What I've learned is goals that aren't rooted in our deepest values will never lead to true fulfillment. Instead of chasing achievement for the sake of achievement, we need to shift our focus to setting goals that are *aligned*—not just *big*. Goals that reflect who we are, what we care about, and the life we actually want to build.

I experienced this firsthand in my business when I set a revenue goal of $250K in my third year of business. At first, it felt exciting and motivating—like proof that my work was growing and my impact was expanding. But as I pushed toward that number, I started making decisions that didn't feel right. I found myself obsessing over conversion rates, strategizing how to scale, and viewing potential clients as numbers on a spreadsheet instead of people I truly wanted to serve. The deeper I got into my pursuit of this goal, the more I felt disconnected from the heart of my work—helping women create sustainable businesses without burning out. The irony wasn't lost on me. In my pursuit of success, I was drifting away from what actually mattered: connection.

That realization forced me to pause and reassess. Instead of focusing solely on hitting $250K, I redefined success through the lens of my values. Connection has always been at the core of my work—genuine relationships, meaningful conversations, and transformation beyond just financial results. So I shifted my goal. Instead of making revenue the primary measure of success, I made it about depth. My new goal became: serve

100 women deeply, with intention, and create an experience where they feel truly seen and supported. The crazy thing? When I leaned into connection, the revenue followed. But more importantly, I felt good about how I was growing my business again.

Values-based goal-setting starts with defining what truly matters to you—not what society, your industry, or even your past self says you *should* care about, but what actually feels right at your core. Your values act as your compass, guiding every decision, every commitment, and every next step. When we set goals from this place of alignment, we don't just check off accomplishments—we build a life and business that feels sustainable, energizing, and deeply satisfying.

My client Tanis beautifully embodies this approach. From the start of her business, Created Mother, Tanis believed she could create community and give generously, no matter her circumstances. With a small social media platform and the ability to sew hot/cold therapy packs and scrunchies, she saw an opportunity to use what she had to make an impact.

In her second year of business, she donated 50% of her September profit to a local food bank. The next year, she gave 100% of her revenue that month to both a food bank and a women's shelter. Wanting to expand her impact beyond a single month, she restructured her give-back model to donate a *minimum* of 10% of her total yearly revenue. In 2024, that generosity grew even more—she gave away 51% of her revenue in cash and product donations to four local women's shelters.

Now, entering her sixth year, Tanis is grateful for the platform her business has given her to give-back in meaningful ways. What started as a business creating comfort-focused products has grown into something even more powerful—a heart-centered company that uplifts both customers and the community. And the best part? Her customers love knowing their purchases help create lasting change.

What does this look like in your life and business? Instead of setting goals based on external measures of success, you start with your values. Get clear on what's most important—whether that's family, freedom, impact, creativity, or something else entirely—and use those values to shape your goals. From there, you make those goals sustainable by ensuring they honour not just work, but also rest and play. You don't need to push harder; you can flow smarter.

Values-based goal-setting is not about achieving more just for the sake of it. It's about creating a life that actually feels good to live. One where your goals reflect your values, your schedule reflects your priorities, and your success is measured not just in milestones, but in how much joy, peace, and presence you experience along the way. Because at the end of the day, the goal isn't just to do more—it's to live fully.

This is where my CEO Flow Goal-Setting Framework comes in. It's about setting goals in three key areas: Being Goals (who you want to be); Doing Goals (what actions align with your values); and Having Goals (what you want to create or experience). And instead of overwhelming ourselves with massive leaps, we take micro-steps—small, intentional actions that build momentum without burning us out. We also recognize that success isn't just about consistency—it's about alignment. If a goal no longer fits the season you're in, you have permission to pivot. You are allowed to change your mind.

For the following exercise, copy this framework in your own journal and answer the questions there.

CEO Flow Goal-Setting Framework

Values-based goals feel aligned, not overwhelming. The CEO Flow Goal-Setting Framework helps you set goals in three key areas:

Being Goals → Who do you want to *be*?
Doing Goals → What actions align with your values?
Having Goals → What do you want to create or experience?

Step 1: Define Your Values
What truly matters to you? In your journal, write your top three values.

Step 2: Set Your CEO Flow Goals
For each of the three areas, be clear about your goals:

Being Goal: Who you want to be
Example: A present and engaged leader
My Goal:

Doing Goal: Actions that align with your values
Example: Block off one CEO day per month
My Goal:

Having Goal: What you want to create/experience
Example: A business that supports rest and freedom
My Goal:

Step 3: Take One Micro-Step
What's one small step you can schedule this week?

Example: Set a 4-day workweek boundary
My Step:

True success isn't just about doing more—it's about building a life that *feels good* to live.

Ditch the To-Do List

Now that you've created some goals, it's time to learn the power of making decisions ahead of time through scheduling. The simple act of planning today what you are going to do tomorrow will give you hours back every single week. By dedicating just 10 to 15 minutes at the end of each workweek to outline and prioritize tasks for the following week, you can start the next work week with a clear focus, increased efficiency, and reduced decision fatigue. This proactive approach allows you to stay organized, create a clear roadmap for success, and ultimately save time throughout your week. Let me show you how.

Most of us take one of two approaches to managing our time:

1. We create a long to-do list that overwhelms us every time we look at it, and never actually gets done. This is the

strategy I see most of my clients using and though the intention is there, the strategy isn't effective.
2. We don't make any plans at all and live in reaction to the circumstances that present themselves each day. Let's be honest, this isn't really a strategy at all.

It's no wonder that most of us feel like there is never enough time. It's because the time we have isn't being used with intentionality.

If you want to live a rested life, it's time to try another approach. This way is not about reacting, nor is it about constantly trying to keep up with a never-ending to-do list. The third option, and the way that will help you master your time once and for all, is scheduling.

Right away there are some of you who hear the word "schedule" and immediately feel trapped. You're spontaneous, you're fun, and you like to go with the flow. I hear you. But stick with me, okay? What if I told you that having a schedule can actually create *more* opportunity for you to be spontaneous *and* make sure the things that matter most to you still get done?

Our brains are not designed for to-do lists. To-do lists require our brain to store a bunch of information instead of processing it. According to cognitive load theory, our brains have limited capacity for information processing, and when we keep tasks in our minds without committing to them, it increases cognitive load, leading to mental fatigue and decreased productivity. To-do lists are essentially unmade decisions, and whenever we have an unmade decision in our mind, it's a drain on our energy. Science backs this up showing that unmade decisions consume mental energy, similar to a running tap that requires action to turn off. In order to close the tap, we need to make the decision, and to make the decision, we need to get it off our list and onto the calendar. This approach helps reduce mental fatigue and allows for more effective decision-making and emotional regulation.

When we look at our to-do list to start off our work day and try to decide what to do first, it's often hard to decide in the moment. You've been there, right? Sitting in your office, looking at that long list and feeling overwhelmed. And instead of making a clear decision we end up scrolling Instagram. Come on—I know I'm not the only one.

But when we shift to a schedule instead of a to-do list, we make the decisions instead of leaving them unmade. Not only do we make the decisions, we make them ahead of time. This is the key. Instead of making decisions in the moment, we start making them in advance.

When we make decisions in the moment, we use our primitive brain and our primitive brain has three main functions: (1) avoid pain, (2) seek pleasure, and (3) be as efficient as possible. When we make decisions from this place, we aren't really thinking about creating the life we want in the long term. We aren't thinking about how to keep rest as the priority. We're just thinking about what's the easiest thing, with the least amount of discomfort, I can do right now. And as you know, the easiest, least comfortable tasks are not usually the ones that move us towards our big goals and dreams.

But when we make decisions ahead of time, we use our prefrontal cortex. This is the part of our brain that can think about how our decisions today are going to affect our life tomorrow, next month, and in five years from now. This part of our brain can prioritize our value for rest and use it as a filter to make decisions about how we allot our time for the week ahead. This is the part of the brain we want running the show when it comes to mastering our time.

So how do we do this? I've created a process called the **Weekly Power Hour** which I teach in depth in my coaching membership, CEO Flow. Because I know the power of this exercise and I really want you to succeed, I'm sharing some of it here with you.

The Weekly Power Hour System

1. Set aside an hour to plan your week.
2. Write out a to-do list of everything you want to get done in the coming week, both personally and professionally.
3. Look at the list and prioritize what tasks are most important to move you towards your current goals. Be willing to remove items off your list that aren't truly aligned with your values or feel like shoulds.
4. Schedule your rest time first! Put it into your calendar. Time to read, walk, connect with loved ones, stare at the horizon. This must come first.
5. Take the items from the to-do list and put them into your calendar with a specific time block. I like to write my list out on paper and then schedule it electronically, on my phone.
6. When the item has been scheduled into your calendar for the week, cross it off your list.

7. Repeat steps 5 and 6 until all the items have been crossed off.
8. If there are any items that don't fit into your calendar, add them to a "someday maybe" list that you can revisit the next week.
9. Honour your schedule by doing the things you decided to do, at the time you decided to do them.
10. Rinse and repeat next week.

This looks like a pretty straightforward process, right? But the challenge comes when you start your week and things don't go as planned. You get an unexpected phone call, the task you planned to do in an hour takes two, or you just don't feel like doing what's on the schedule. I get it. I've been using this system for the past five years and it's still a work in progress. The key thing here is that you learn from what's working and what's not working, and to make adjustments each week. I promise if you commit to this process, it will give you hours back every single day. All the time you used to spend in indecision, you can now invest into rest, play, and work.

Why does this system work so well? Because you do the heavy lifting of the decision making during your planning session instead of in the moment each day. And when you decide ahead of time, it's much more likely that you will actually follow through. This is how we work from rest. We learn to stop flying by the seat of our pants and be intentional about how we invest our hours each day. This is what it looks like to be a rested woman. She has a plan, and her plan is helping her create the life she truly wants. And that is pretty darn sexy if you ask me.

Slow Down and Surrender

We generally view time as a limited resource and feel compelled to use it productively. This mindset can make it difficult to justify rest without feeling guilty about potentially "wasting time." But the truth is, we all have enough time for what matters most to us. What we don't have time for is feeling guilty for living a life aligned with our values. That BS has got to stop. We are wasting our precious time trying to meet an impossible standard of productivity and perfection. Rest isn't a waste of time, it's an investment of time. Rest isn't something to feel guilty about, it's something to feel proud of. The next time you stop to take mental, emotional, or physical rest, remind yourself of the powerful thought you created earlier (e.g. there *is* enough time).

Instead of always rushing from one thing to the next, what if we were to slow down? What if we approached our life more like a marathon rather than a sprint? What would happen? I work with many female founders who run their own companies and when I ask them this question, they often answer by saying "the projects wouldn't get done" or "the deadlines wouldn't be met." My response to them is "What if we change the deadline then? You're the one making them in the first place."

Most of the things that we feel are urgent, aren't actually urgent at all. The truth is we are all just making up deadlines and then holding them over our own heads! We're doing it to ourselves. Maybe you're thinking, "But the client wants it by this date," or "My boss said it had to be done by such-and-such time." Guess what, just because someone asks for something doesn't mean we have to agree with it! We get to choose. And when we are choosing from rest, we don't give up on the goal, we simply extend the timeline. If you find yourself always rushing to meet a deadline, make sure you give yourself more time on the next project! It really is that simple.

If you knew you had enough time to accomplish everything your heart desired to do, how would that change your relationship with rest?

The other day I was sitting on my front porch, reflecting on my life and what I have accomplished so far (midlife vibes over here). I found myself feeling behind. Internally I started listing all the things I thought I would have done by now that I hadn't. I should have made a million dollars in my business, served thousands of women through my coaching, been given more opportunities to speak and teach to larger audiences, grown my social media following, and on and on.

As the chatter quieted and I gazed up at the sky, a phrase surfaced in my mind: *"The timeline is the playground of the ego. The present is the playground of the soul."*

The more I reflected on these words, the lighter I felt. Of course, the ego pushes us to race against the clock, chasing accomplishments to validate our worth. Of course, it whispers that we're falling behind. But the deepest, truest part of me—my soul—knows a different truth. It knows I don't have to measure my life by speed or accomplishment. I can simply sink into the gift of the present moment and just *be*. This present moment is all that we have. And that is a gift.

High Intention, Low Attachment

So how do we stay connected to the present, and not caught up in the timeline? How do we practice contentment and still dream big? High intention and low attachment. This is a phrase I live by that keeps me connected to my worthiness, and to rest. It keeps me showing up in a big way, while also enabling me to sleep peacefully at night even when there is more to be done. So what does this phrase even mean? I choose to have high intentions in the areas where I have control—my thoughts, feelings, and actions—and low attachment in the areas where I don't have control—the outcome of my efforts.

A powerful example of high intention, low attachment in my life was when I applied for a business contest put on by Amy Porterfield. At the time, my business was struggling, and I felt like I needed a big break. I put my heart into my application, sharing my vision and why my work mattered. I set the high intention to show up fully, give my best effort, and trust that my story would resonate. But I also reminded myself that the outcome—whether I won or not—was out of my hands. When I got the email saying I had won $1,000, it wasn't just about the money; it was confirmation that I was on the right path. And even if I hadn't won, I gained something valuable— the confidence that I was willing to bet on myself. This is the power of high intention and low attachment. It allows us to dream big and take bold action, while staying grounded in the present, knowing our worth isn't tied to any single result.

Even though it's hard to let go of the timing of things and exactly how they will all turn out, it's what allows us to rest. It's what keeps the high achieving woman with big dreams from burning herself out. It's what has helped me grow a six-figure business in two and a half days a week, create courses, speak at events, coach hundreds of women while raising a family of five and being present in my marriage and for myself. It's not because I have it all together—I surely do not. But when I learned to be intentional in the areas I have control and surrender and rest in the ones I don't that is when things really started to get fun.

Action Step: Practice High Intention, Low Attachment

This week, choose one goal or project where you can practice high intention and low attachment.

1. **Set a High Intention.** Identify what's in your control: your effort, mindset, and the way you show up. Define a clear action step you can take with full commitment.
2. **Release Attachment to the Outcome.** Remind yourself that while you can influence the process, the final result is beyond your control. Write down an affirmation like: *"I will show up fully, but my worth is not determined by the outcome."*
3. **Reflect and Adjust.** At the end of the week, take five minutes to reflect: How did it feel to hold both intention and surrender? What shifted in your energy, stress levels, or ability to rest?

By consistently practising this mindset, you'll begin to experience the freedom that comes from taking bold action without burnout.

CHAPTER 11

Burnout-Proof Your Life

Burnout is such a hot topic right now. I'm guessing that either you or someone you know is experiencing burnout, on their way to it, or trying to find their way out of it. And it's a place that none of us wants to be. I've been there myself as I shared earlier in the book and my hope is that you never have to experience it.

Burnout is different from just being tired, stressed, or overwhelmed. Burnout is the result of being tired, stressed, or overwhelmed for months or even years at a time. That prolonged state of exhaustion is what causes the experience of burnout. And just like it takes months or years to get there, it takes more than a few days or weeks to heal from it.

Many of the strategies we've talked about in this book can help you heal from burnout. But more than anything I want you to be equipped with the tools to prevent burnout from happening. Here's what you need to know.

What causes burnout isn't the number of events on your calendar or how long you're to-do list is. The core of burnout is the people-pleasing that is driven by our own feelings of unworthiness. I define people-pleasing as doing things we don't want to do, because we believe other people want us to do them. Living this way may sound selfless, but it comes at a cost. Every time we say yes when we really mean no, we break down our relationship of trust with ourselves. We send a message to our brain that everyone else matters and that we don't really matter.

This constant state of overriding our desire and intuition is a form of gaslighting ourselves. It's rooted in the same thing we've been talking about this whole book—unworthiness. But when we truly start to believe that we are worthy, and that we don't have to be productive to earn or prove our worthiness, we aren't only creating a more rested life, we are most importantly creating a burnout-proof life.

When you believe you are worthy, it doesn't take away from someone else's worthiness. Instead of saying, "you matter and I don't," we say, "we all matter." What you want matters and what I want matters too. The first step to break up with people-pleasing is to start believing that you matter. That your wants and needs matter. That if helping someone else comes at the expense of your relationship with yourself, the cost is too high.

Here are three practical ways you can burnout-proof your life:

1. Prioritize Self-Care

Self-care is crucial for maintaining physical, emotional, and mental rest. Self-care looks like taking intentional actions to nurture yourself: body, mind, and heart. Here are some specific ways to prioritize self-care in your daily life:

- *Regular Exercise*: Move your body every day! Choose physical activities you actually enjoy, whether it's walking, yoga, swimming, or weightlifting. Regular exercise reduces stress and boosts overall well-being. My husband and I recently took up pickleball and I've gotta say, the hype is real. It's been so fun to find an activity we can do together that doesn't require us to be an expert. Although our instructor Chris is pretty convinced we could go pro if we keep at it.

- *Healthy Eating*: Girl - you gotta eat your protein! I've been on a protein journey lately and it has been so eye opening. This isn't a nutrition book, but do your research, hire a health coach, and eat your dang protein. We all know that proper nutrition fuels our body and mind. I recommend using some kind of macro tracking app or program. I've found tracking macros gives me the freedom to still have ice cream or cookies occasionally (or every other day!) and still get great results.

- *Adequate Sleep*: Going to bed early is the new staying up late! For real. Aim for 7-8 hours of quality sleep per night. Good sleep hygiene, such as maintaining a consistent sleep schedule, limiting screen use before bed, and creating a restful environment, is really helpful.

- *Mindfulness and Relaxation Techniques*: Practice mindfulness, meditation, or deep-breathing exercises to reduce stress and increase mental clarity. I love using the Headspace app to do a simple ten-minute meditation, especially on days when my head feels foggy or my anxiety is high.

2. Set Boundaries

One of the biggest things that keeps us from rest is our addiction to people-pleasing. A practical first step to breaking this addiction is to set healthy boundaries. Here are some practical steps to set those boundaries, starting with the most important one: *Learn to Say No.*

This is a big one and it's hard to tackle in a paragraph or two. But here's a practical approach to saying no that can be especially helpful when you're feeling overwhelmed. If you want additional support on implementing this, I would highly recommend working with a coach.

- *Start with Your Values*
  Take a moment to revisit the value list you created earlier. These values represent what matters most to you—your guiding principles, the things that fuel your sense of purpose. Now, make a list of all the commitments you currently have, both personal and professional. This can include family obligations, work responsibilities, social events, volunteer work, and anything else you've said yes to.

- *Assess Each Commitment*
  It's important to be honest with yourself. If something doesn't align with your values or drains you, it might be time to let go. Think about the emotional energy required to maintain each commitment. Is it worth it? Look at each commitment and ask yourself:
    - Does this align with my values?
    - Does this align with the vision I have for my life?
    - Does this bring me energy or drain me?

- *Evaluate Your Capacity*
Consider your current mental, emotional, and physical capacity. We all have limits. If you're already stretched thin, saying yes to anything additional could compromise your ability to show up as your best self in other areas of your life. Ask yourself, "Do I have the time, energy, and space to take this on right now?"

- *Create Your "Yes" List*
This is where the magic happens. When you learn to say no, you actually make space for the things that truly matter. Take a moment to list the commitments that align with your values and bring you joy or fulfillment. This will become your "yes" list. Every time you say yes to something, ask yourself if it belongs on this list. If not, it might be a no.

- *Practice Saying No*
Saying no can feel uncomfortable, especially if you're used to saying yes all the time. But it's important to remember: *their reaction is not your responsibility*. People may be disappointed, frustrated, or even upset when you say no, but that's a reflection of their needs, not yours. It's okay to say no, and it actually strengthens the value of your yes. When you reserve your yes for things that align with your values and true desires, you give it more meaning.

For example, let's say you've been asked to take on a new project at work. If this new project doesn't align with your values—perhaps it conflicts with spending more time with family, or it doesn't resonate with your career goals—then it might be time to decline politely. You could say something like, "I really appreciate the opportunity, but after careful consideration, I'm going to pass on this one to focus on [your top priority]." By doing this, you are not only preserving your energy but also honouring your boundaries and your values.

Remember, saying no doesn't make you selfish—it makes you self-aware. It's an act of self-care that allows you to show up in a more authentic and aligned way. Your commitments should reflect the life you want to create, not the life that others expect from you.

- *Schedule Breaks:* When you are doing the Weekly Power Hour, make sure to schedule breaks in the day to rest and recharge. This includes short breaks during work day to eat, stretch, or go for a walk. Don't forget about scheduling longer periods of time off for vacations as a family, with your partner, or even alone! Yes, taking a trip alone can be a healthy way to prevent burnout.

- *Delegate and Ask for Help*: Delegate tasks to other skilled people. You don't have to do it all! Find someone who is even better at the task than you are, and hire them, or ask for their help. Collaboration and shared responsibilities lighten the load. So many of us struggle to ask for help because we feel a sense of over-responsibility. But remember, asking for help is agreeing with your worthiness.

- *Manage Work Hours*: Avoid excessive overtime by setting clear boundaries between work and personal life. Create specific work hours while doing your power hour and stick to them. This is especially important if you run an online business from your phone. Communicate your office hours to your clients and don't expect others to honour them more than you do.

3. Cultivate a Supportive Environment

A supportive environment, both at work and in your personal life, is vital for preventing burnout. This includes building strong relationships and creating a positive atmosphere:

- *Foster Positive Relationships*: Surround yourself with supportive and positive people who encourage and uplift you. Engage in social activities that you enjoy. And for your own self-love, stop spending time with people you don't actually enjoy being with. If a person is constantly triggering your nervous system, it's okay to take space away from them. Prioritize relationships that help you feel regulated and safe.

- *Seek Professional Support*: When you feel overwhelmed or stuck in a loop, ask for help from a therapist or certified coach. Professional guidance can provide strategies for managing stress and maintaining mental health. I personally love having at least one coach and therapist on call at any given time.

- *Create a Restful Work Environment*: Organize your workspace to be comfortable and inspiring. Personalize it with items that make you happy and reduce clutter to minimize stress. Light a candle, burn some incense, or play music you love. I recently found this amazing hand soap from Aesop called Reverence and every time I use it, the smell brings me so much joy!

- *Have Fun*: Pursue hobbies and interests that bring you joy and fulfillment. Engaging in meaningful activities outside of work provides a sense of purpose and balance. When was the last time you did something, just for fun? Join a dance class, plan a painting party, or go skinny dipping!

Implementing even just one or two of these simple strategies can help you build resilience against burnout and enhance your overall quality of life. But remember, *none* of these activities on their own will bring you rest. Rest is an inside job. It starts with you loving and supporting yourself. Many of these suggestions will be the overflow that comes as you build a relationship of trust with yourself. Please don't read this list and get overwhelmed, but rather use it as inspiration for where you are headed.

Your Rest Plan

If you truly want to burnout-proof your life, don't wait for next week or next month. Don't wait for January, the first of the month, or a Monday. Start today. I want to challenge you to create your own rest plan.

Consider the rhythms of rest you can incorporate daily, weekly, monthly, and annually.

Here are some ideas. As you read them over, pay attention to the ones that resonate with you the most and start to create your rest plan. Remember that the best way to take action from rest is to make a plan ahead of time. In your journal write down the one thing you're going to try each day, week, month, and year for this year.

Daily Rest Ideas

1. Morning routine (I'm giving mine away for free at heatherboersma.com)
2. Meditation break
3. Power nap
4. Read for pleasure
5. Gentle exercise
6. Phone-free time
7. Breathing exercise
8. Quiet time
9. Enjoy a hobby
10. Hot bath
11. Gratitude journal
12. Kitchen dance party
13. Cup of tea or coffee
14. Listen to music
15. Morning stretch
16. Visualization exercises
17. Aromatherapy
18. Mindful eating
19. Sunlight break
20. Watch something that makes you laugh

Weekly Rest Ideas

1. Digital detox day
2. Nature walks
3. Face mask
4. Family time
5. Cooking or baking
6. Art and creativity
7. Music and relaxation
8. Coffee date
9. Sleep-In day
10. Journaling
11. Picnic in the park
12. Board games
13. Visit a museum
14. Bubble bath
15. Gardening
16. Attend a concert
17. Photography walk
18. Soak in a hot tub
19. DIY project
20. Explore a new area

Monthly Rest Ideas

1. Weekend getaway
2. Staycation
3. Massage therapy
4. Get a facial
5. Movie marathon
6. Take a workshop or class
7. Creative retreat

8. Reconnect with friends
9. Self-reflection
10. Day trip
11. Book club
12. Yin Yoga class
13. Cultural event
14. Cooking class
15. Home spa day
16. Beach day
17. Mindfulness workshop
18. Explore nature
19. Therapy appointment
20. Girls' night

Annual Rest Ideas

1. Vacation with friends
2. Vacation with partner
3. Solo vacation
4. Wellness retreat
5. Annual health check
6. Family adventure
7. Personal retreat
8. Holiday festivities
9. Room refresh
10. Annual hobby day
11. Professional development
12. Nature adventure
13. Yoga retreat
14. Camping off the grid
15. Stargazing

Experiment with Rest

The above lists are not about just another "thing to-do." These lists are about reminding yourself of the power of rest. Or if you're still not convinced, using it as an experiment with rest. One of the best ways to build the evidence your brain needs to believe that rest is actually powerful is to try it and see what happens.

I did an experiment like this while writing this book. I was working on a deadline to get the second draft of the book to my publisher. Earlier in the day, she had emailed and asked if I could have the second draft to her in two days time. I was at 18000 words and aiming for 20000 and said, "sure!" Even though I had so many other things going on that week, I went to my husband and told him I was going to write that evening. He asked me "how many words and for how long?"

"One thousand words or two hours, whatever comes first," I replied.

"One thousand words or one hour," he countered. "I'll set a timer and come get you at 8pm. I'm starting the timer now."

An hour later he knocked on my office door as I was finishing up my 891st word.

"That's time," he said, as he gently closed my laptop.

A part of me wanted to resist because I hadn't hit my 1000 word target. But then he reminded me of my own words.

"If you stop now and sleep on it, you'll have even more to write in the morning." And wouldn't you know it, I woke up at 7am the next day, and while the kids slept, finished writing the 1000 words I set out to write the night before, plus another 1000.

The way to burnout-proof our lives is to prioritize rest, even when it seems logical to keep working. To push through for another hour, but not for two. And to trust that our best work often happens when we set aside our work and allow our brain and body time to recalibrate and rest.

CHAPTER 12

Rest Is the Revolution

I told myself I wasn't going to write another book. After completing the first two, I realized that book writing is not the glamorous job one imagines it to be. After completing my second book, I decided the *only* way I would ever write another book is if an idea was *burning* in my heart and would not leave me alone. And thanks to Elizabeth Gilbert and her wisdom and perspective, an idea found me and would not leave me alone.

I went to see Elizabeth speak in the spring of 2023. On top of being refreshingly honest and disarmingly funny, she also shared an idea that put words to something I'd been feeling for years. What she said was essentially this (and I'm paraphrasing): "The revolution is no longer the badass women. The revolution is the relaxed woman." When I heard that something inside of me jumped up and screamed, "yes!" Working as a life and business coach for female entrepreneurs, I've been immersed in the world of badass boss babes for years, and to be honest, I'm over it. And many of the women in that world are completely exhausted. Maybe you're one of them. I know I was.

Between the day I got the idea for this book and the day I submitted my first draft, a year later, was one of the hardest years of my life. It was the year my marriage almost ended. It was the year my business made less money than it had since I launched it. It was the year I broke my ankle as I was working towards a goal of being the strongest I'd been at forty. It was the year I was told my breast MRI was not clear, and I would need to have a biopsy that may show I had breast cancer. It was a year where it would have made sense to hustle and grind to try to make everything that was falling apart, stay together.

But because of all the lessons of rest I'd learned in the previous ten years, I chose not to hustle. I chose to surrender. And rest didn't look like relaxation at all. It looked like letting go. It looked like choosing to go for a walk on the beach even when I couldn't pay my $17,000 tax bill. It looked like taking up the practice of hot yoga instead of doing another HIIT workout. It looked like investing thousands of dollars in marriage therapy even though less money was coming into my business. It looked like not giving up even when I felt completely hopeless. It felt radical to rest when everything was falling apart. But it's this approach that helped me stay connected to myself and come out on the other side.

Today my marriage is better than ever before (the story of that is a whole other book). Today my business is building back up to where it was before, and I paid my tax bill the day I got it. Today my ankle is healed and I have a clean bill of health. But all that feels less important compared to the level of trust and support I have with myself because I chose to approach it all from rest—never questioning my worthiness, despite how hard my circumstances got.

This is the revolution. It's the revolution of, not just the relaxed woman, but the *rested woman.* The relaxed woman moves slowly, stares at the horizon, and takes breaks when she needs. But the *rested woman* is grounded deeply in the knowledge of her worth no matter how the storms of life rages around her. Some days she moves slowly, but other days she drives hard towards her goal, *from* a place of inner rest. It's not about high productivity vs. low productivity. It's about high self-worth vs. low self-worth. The rested woman knows who she is and because of that relationship of trust with herself, she knows when to go hard and when to rest.

I want my children to remember me as a rested woman. I want them to have memories of me being present, reading a good book on the porch, and enjoying a slow morning with a hot cup of coffee. But I also want them to remember me pursuing my dreams with a relentless passion, not because I was desperate or striving, but because I was overflowing from the inside out. I don't want one or the other. I want both. This is the revolution of rest.

The action we take doesn't matter as much as the energy it's coming from. Hustle isn't about a busy schedule. It's about abandoning ourselves for the sake of that schedule. And rest isn't about lying around all the time. It's about prioritizing a regulated nervous system, processing our emotions, and managing our minds. My hope for you after reading this book is that you feel drawn to start living *from rest*. This is the revolution, my friend. It's you living your one precious life to the fullest, from a place of deep rest inside.

What if we stopped thinking of rest in opposition to our dreams and started to believe that rest is actually the pathway to making those dreams a reality? That it isn't about being lazy or irresponsible, but about allowing our bodies and minds to produce something beautiful, without our conscious effort. To trust that the greatness we are about to give birth to is actually being formed in our rest. This is the revolution.

It doesn't mean we pull back or check out or take our foot of the gas. It means we trust that there is a force bigger than ourselves, working on our behalf. Call it God, or love, or the universe—it's the mystery of life that no matter what we do, or how hard we try, we can't control the outcome. And though this may be frustrating, it's something I resisted for a long time, it's actually where we find the freedom to rest. Freedom comes when we realize that there is only so much we can control, and it's not pushing or forcing or striving that creates the result. It's actually in surrender that magic happens.

If this resonates with you, I invite you to join the revolution. Reading this book is just the starting line and it's a very good place to start. Even though you may not have taken a physical step towards rest yet, you now have the mindset to motivate you and the steps to take. Here's a reminder of the steps to take:

The Steps to Rest:

1. Regulate your Nervous System
2. Think Powerful Thoughts
3. Feel your Feelings
4. Live FROM not FOR

If you're looking for some powerful thoughts to practice to start living a lifestyle of rest, I've written a Rest Manifesto for us to practice.

The Rest Manifesto

As a rested woman I choose to:

- live FROM love, not FOR it
- say no when the opportunities aren't aligned with my values
- take time for myself even if others don't understand it
- prioritize nervous system regulation
- think powerful thoughts that serve me
- feel my feelings even when it's uncomfortable
- dream big dreams and pursue them with heart rather than hustle
- live with high intentions and low attachment

The Rest Revolution is a quiet one. It doesn't have to look like masses of women storming the castle of productivity to take it down with effort and might. It looks like a woman choosing to sit on her couch and read a good book rather than clean up the dishes on the counter.

It looks like an afternoon nap on a rainy Sunday afternoon when there is laundry to be done and baseboards that need dusting.

The Rest Revolution happens every time you choose to check in with your true desires instead of should-ing yourself.

It happens in the moments no one sees when you stop and put a hand over your anxious, racing heart and take a moment to do the long exhale rather than simply rushing to the next thing.

I knew I was a part of this revolution when one of my most energetic, productive friends said she was "pulling a Heather" by taking a moment to rest in her bed even though her to-do list was calling.

I want to be one of the women remembered for not how hard she hustled, but how well she rested.

And I want that for you too.

Will you join me?

RESOURCES

Here are some of the studies and experts I've mentioned:

Books & Authors:

Deb Dana– *Anchored: How to Befriend Your Nervous System Using Polyvagal Theory.* (2021) Sounds True Publishing.

Elizabeth Gilbert – Author of both fiction and nonfiction. Her book *Big Magic: Creative Living Without Fear* (2015) and her newsletter, as well as interviews, offer inspiring guidance on how to embrace life.

Dr. Caroline Leaf – Expert in cognitive neuroscience. *Switch on Your Brain: The Key to Peak Happiness, Thinking, and Health* (2016) and *Think Learn Succeed: Understanding and Unlocking the Power of the Brain* (2017).

Hillary L. McBride – *The Wisdom of Your Body: Finding Healing, Wholeness, and Connection through Embodied Living* (2021), Harper Collins.

Kristin Neff – *Self-Compassion: The Proven Power of Being Kind to Yourself* (2015), William Marrow Paperbacks.

Studies & Research:

Bergland, C. (2024)."Longer Exhalations Are an Easy Way to Hack Your Vagus Nerve." *Psychology Today*. May 20, 2024.

Bolte Taylor, J. (2021). *Whole Brain Living: The Anatomy of Choice and the Four Characters That Drive Our Life.* Hayhouse.

Deci, E. L., & Ryan, R. M. (2000). "The "What" and "Why" of Goal Pursuits: Human Needs and the Self-Determination of Behavior." *Psychological Inquiry*, 11(4), 227–268.

Dufresne, S. F., Aubertin, M., & Lajoie, S. (2023). "The demographic features of fatigue in the general population worldwide: A systematic review and meta-analysis." *Frontiers in Public Health*, 11, 1192121.

Patton, K. & Thibodeau, G. (2016). *The Human Body in Health and Disease.* Elsevier.

Petersen, A. H. (2019). *How millennials became the burnout generation.* BuzzFeed News. https://www.buzzfeednews.com/article/annehelenpetersen/millennials-burnout-generation-debt-work

Pinel, J. & Barnes, S. (2020). *Biopsychology, 11th Edition.* Pearson Education.

Sweller, J., Ayres, P., & Kalyuga, S. (2011). *Cognitive Load Theory.* Springer Science & Business Media.

Vlasceanu, M., McMahon, C. E., Van Bavel, J. J., & Coman, A. (2023). "Political and Nonpolitical Belief Change Elicits Behavioral Change." *Psychological Science*, 34(5), 678–688.

Werner, K. H., Jazaieri, H., Goldin, P. R., Ziv, M., Heimberg, R. G., & Gross, J. J. (2012). "Self-compassion and social anxiety disorder." *Anxiety, stress, and coping*, 25(5), 543–558.

ACKNOWLEDGEMENTS

I told myself I wasn't going to write another book, but then I heard Elizabeth Gilbert talk about *the relaxed woman*, and this book idea was born. Something in me knew I had to write it—not just for myself, but for every woman who's ever felt like she had to do it all, hold it all, and still smile through it.

This book wouldn't exist without the people who supported, inspired, and walked beside me through every stage of the process.

To my clients: You are the heartbeat behind this message. Your courage, honesty, and commitment to growth inspire me daily. Thank you for trusting me with your stories and letting me walk alongside you in your work/life journey. This book was written with you in mind and heart.

To my husband, Alex: Thank you for believing in me—even in the moments I doubted myself. Your quiet strength, consistent support, and willingness to do your own inner work inspire me more than you know. I'm so grateful we're building this life together.

To Cohen, Claire, and Byron: Thank you for living out the wow's and pow's with me every single day. You are my greatest teachers, my biggest joy, and the reason I care so deeply about emotional health and legacy. I love you endlessly.

To The Self Publishing Agency—especially Megan and Ira: Thank you for guiding me through this process with professionalism, warmth, and enthusiasm. Your support helped bring this dream to life.

To Judith, my editor: Your words came exactly when I needed them most. When I felt like giving up, your encouragement reminded me that this message matters. Thank you for seeing the heart behind every sentence.

To Jess: Thank you for always answering when I call—whether I'm on the verge of tears or celebrating a win. Your presence is a lifeline, and I'm so thankful to have you in my corner.

To Amanda: So many of the ideas in this book were born and refined in our FaceTime calls and in-person visits. Thank you for being a sounding board, a truth-teller, and a safe space to dream out loud. Your friendship is woven into every chapter.

And to Alisha: For almost 25 years, you've been the kind of friend who makes me feel like I can do anything. Your belief in me has never wavered, and I'm endlessly grateful to have you by my side through every season.

To everyone who helped shape this book with your love, wisdom, and encouragement—thank you. You've given me the courage to share my voice, and I hope this book gives others the same.

ABOUT THE AUTHOR

Heather Boersma is a speaker, coach, and author who helps ambitious women create sustainable success by finding their flow—not their limit. With over 15 years of experience empowering women through speaking, writing, and coaching, Heather brings a unique blend of neuroscience, emotional health, and lived experience to her work.

She is the founder of the *CEO Flow Membership*, host of retreats and workshops across North America, and the voice behind a growing online community that encourages women to slow down, soften, and live more intentionally. Her honest and practical approach is grounded in her own journey through motherhood, entrepreneurship, and personal healing—including living with the BRCA2 gene mutation.

Heather is currently completing her Master of Counselling Psychology to deepen her work at the intersection of emotional health and sustainable success. She lives in Vancouver, BC with her husband Alex and their three children—Cohen, Claire, and Byron—who are daily reminders of the beauty in the "wow's and pow's" of life. Whether she's coaching a client, speaking on stage, or writing at her kitchen table, Heather's mission remains the same: to help women build lives and businesses they don't need to escape from.

CEO Flow:
The Next Right Step After The Rest Revolution

Reading The Rest Revolution changes the way you think. CEO Flow changes the way you live.

If *The Rest Revolution* helped you wake up to the unsustainable pace of your life, *CEO Flow* is your invitation to do something about it. This powerful program is the bridge between **passive action**—gaining insight, shifting your mindset—and **massive action**, where real, lasting transformation happens.

In *CEO Flow*, you'll stop just *learning* about balance and start *living* it. Through coaching, accountability, and a supportive community, you'll create the kind of work/life rhythm that fuels your ambition without burning you out.

In CEO Flow, you'll:
- Implement the rest-based routines and scheduling strategies from *The Rest Revolution*.
- Create a personalized plan for your work, rest, and play so your calendar actually reflects your values.
- Get live coaching to overcome the mindset blocks that keep you stuck in hustle mode.
- Connect with other ambitious women who are committed to sustainable success.
- Build a life and business that feel as good on the inside as they look on the outside.

It's time to stop consuming information and start taking aligned, intentional *massive action*.

It's time to step into your flow.

www.ingramcontent.com/pod-product-compliance
Lightning Source LLC
Chambersburg PA
CBHW020341010526
44119CB00048B/554